AMERICA'S ENDANGERED BIRDS

AMERICA'S ENDANGERED BIRDS

PROGRAMS AND PEOPLE WORKING TO SAVE THEM

ROBERT M. McCLUNG

ILLUSTRATED BY GEORGE FOUNDS

William Morrow and Company   New York 1979

Library of Congress Cataloging in Publication Data

McClung, Robert M.
  America's endangered birds.

  Bibliography: p.
  Includes index.
  Summary: Examines the plight of six endangered birds, including the bald eagle and California condor, and discusses the latest research on their reproduction.
  1. Birds, Protection of—United States—Juvenile literature. 2. Rare birds—United States—Juvenile literature. [1. Birds—Protection. 2. Rare birds] I. Founds, George. II. Title.
QL676.5.M323 333.9′5 79-9241
ISBN 0-688-22208-0
ISBN 0-688-32208-5 lib. bdg.

Printed in the United States of America.
1 2 3 4 5 6 7 8 9 10

CONTENTS

MAPS

ACKNOWLEDGMENTS

The work of a great many research scientists, wildlife biologists, conservationists and naturalists, and countless books, periodicals, articles, and news items have been consulted in the preparation of this book. Many persons working in programs to help endangered species have generously answered questions, explained details of their research, and furnished me with material. I gratefully acknowledge my indebtedness to all of them. The activities of these people and many others who are engaged in endangered-species research are discussed in the text or listed in the selected bibliography. Without their work, there would be no book.

I am particularly grateful to Ray C. Erickson, Assistant Director for Wildlife Research, Patuxent Wildlife Research Center; Ralph Schreiber, Curator, Ornithology, Los Angeles County Museum of Natural History; and Lovett E. Williams, Jr., Chief, Bureau of Wildlife Research, Florida Game and Fresh Water Fish Commission. They critically read all or portions of the text, and they patiently answered questions that were put to them concerning the entire manuscript. All statements and opinions expressed in the book, unless attributed to others, however, are the sole responsibility of the author, as are any inaccuracies that may be found.

Special thanks are also due the following individuals for their advice and help on particular species or programs: Daniel Anderson, Department of Wildlife and Fisheries, University of California, Davis (western brown pelican); Linda Carlson, Secretary—Science and Research, Florida Audubon Society (ivory-billed woodpecker, Everglade kite); Royce W. Jurries, Wildlife Biologist, Texas Parks and Wildlife Department (Attwater's prairie chicken); Kirke A. King, Research Biologist, Fish and Wildlife Service (eastern brown pelican in Texas); Larry McNease, Biologist, Refuge Division, Louisiana Wildlife and Fisheries Commission (eastern brown pelican in Louisiana); Stephen A. Nesbitt, Wildlife Biologist, Florida Game and Fresh Water Fish Commission (southern bald eagle); David L. Olsen, Division of Wildlife Refuges, Fish and Wildlife Service (whooping crane); John P. O'Neill, Director, Museum of Natural Science, Louisiana State University (ivory-billed woodpecker); Wayne A. Shifflett, Refuge Manager, Attwater Prairie Chicken National Wildlife Refuge (Attwater's prairie chicken); John L. Spinks, Jr., Acting Deputy Associate Director, Fish and Wildlife Service (recovery teams and programs for endangered species); Noel Snyder, Research Biologist, Fish and Wildlife Service (Puerto Rican parrot); Paul W. Sykes, Jr., Wildlife Biologist, Fish and

Wildlife Service (Everglade kite); Sylvia M. Taylor, Co-ordinator, Endangered Species Program, Department of Natural Resources, Michigan (Kirtland's warbler); Lawrence H. Walkinshaw (Kirtland's warbler); Sanford R. Wilbur, Wildlife Research Biologist, Fish and Wildlife Service (California condor); Phil Wilkinson, South Carolina Wildlife and Marine Resources Department, Non-game Endangered Species Section (eastern brown pelican); Stanley N. Wiemeyer, Wildlife Biologist (Research), Patuxent Wildlife Research Center (bald eagle).

FOREWORD

In 1875, a hunter shot the last recorded Labrador duck—
a pretty little black-and-white bird, which had ranged across
America's northeastern coastal areas. In 1914, the last passenger pigeon, an old female named Martha, died in her
cage at the Cincinnati Zoo; only a century before, her ancestors had traveled across America in flocks that numbered
in the billions, their wings roaring like thunder, their
bodies darkening the sky. That same year the last Carolina
parakeet also died in captivity. In 1932, the last heath hen,
an eastern race of the greater prairie chicken, died on Martha's Vineyard. Henry Beetle Hough, editor of the *Vineyard
Gazette*, marked its passing with an oft-quoted comment:
"We are looking upon the utmost finality which can be
written, glimpsing the darkness which will not know an-

other ray of light. We are in touch with the reality of extinction."

We will never again see the likes of those four birds. They are gone forever. How many others will go down that same trail to oblivion? The Eskimo curlew is one probable candidate, if indeed it has not already disappeared. Another victim of overshooting, it was considered extinct in the 1930s, but then two specimens were sighted in 1945. A further lone bird was seen in 1959, two more in 1962, and one was actually shot in 1963. In 1972, another two specimens were sighted on Martha's Vineyard, and still another two in Ontario in 1976. Were these birds really the last Eskimo curlews? The ivory-billed woodpecker may be extinct, too, but the search for it goes on.

The number of species threatened with extinction has increased by leaps and bounds. Man, with his destruction of suitable habitat, his penchant for dousing the Earth with pesticides and other poisons, has seen to that. At the present time, the United States Fish and Wildlife Service lists no fewer than sixty-seven birds native to the United States in danger of extinction, along with thirty-three mammals, sixteen reptiles and amphibians, and twenty-nine fish. How many will be listed in that category in the year 2000? How many will be extinct?

"At the present rate of human exploitation, most of the Earth's major ecosystems will be fragmented during the next twenty-five years," declares William Conway, General Director of the New York Zoological Society. "Much of the world's most beautiful and inspiring wildlife will be lost. This quite thinkable possibility is beginning to stimulate extraordinarily diverse and often bizarre efforts to preserve vanishing animals. Such programs do not treat the ultimate cause of wildlife endangerment; they deal with the symptoms—the loss of animal species. Yet the act of preservation can be a powerful incentive for man to reconsider environmental destruction."

More and more programs are being undertaken every year to help threatened and endangered wildlife. Some of these efforts, like the steps taken years ago to help the trumpeter swan, will succeed; others will almost certainly fail. But, at the very least, nearly all of them will borrow additional time for threatened species.

This book traces the historical background of some threatened or endangered birds and attempts to explain how and why their numbers dwindled. It examines some of the programs that have been undertaken to help them and sketches the valiant efforts of many dedicated organizations and individuals in behalf of the birds. Dr. Dillon S. Ripley, Secretary of the Smithsonian Institution, has noted that "A sense of kinship with nature and a single-mindedness of purpose appear to be the touchstones of success in this work."

1

THE WHOOPING CRANE, SYMBOL OF WILDLIFE CONSERVATION

A loud trumpeting sounds from the sky as seven cranes circle over a wide stretch of coastal marsh and tidal flats. Inland lie grassy meadows broken by pockets of brush and many small ponds. The area is part of the Aransas National Wildlife Refuge on the Texas Gulf Coast.

Spiraling downward, the big birds prepare to land. Braking with their wings, long, sooty legs extended forward, they touch ground gently and run a few steps before stopping. The first two families of whooping cranes have finished the last lap of their 2500-mile journey from their nesting grounds in Canada to their winter territory.

Across the brushlands, the sun sinks low in the western sky as the tall birds begin to forage for food. They probe for crabs in the shallow waters and pick up worms and other tidbits with their long, powerful beaks. These seven birds are two mated pairs—one with a pair of youngsters, the other with just one offspring.

Standing five feet tall and weighing upwards of twenty-five pounds, the four adults are imposing birds. Their body feathers are gleaming white, except for the black-tipped wings. Their piercing eyes are yellow, and the bare skin of their head and cheeks is bright red overlaid with black bristles, which sweep back and downward to form an imposing moustache. As big as their parents, the young birds are mottled with dusky grays and browns.

Raising his beak skyward, the male with two offspring utters a challenging bugle: *ker-loooo! ker-lee-oooo!* Then he makes a rush at the other male and tries to drive him away. The attacking male is already starting to stake out a winter feeding territory for himself and his family. Stretching his beak upward, he bugles again and again.

Wildlife conservationists might interpret those cries as a challenge, for over the years the whooping crane has become a symbol of wildlife conservation in America. It has hovered on the edge of extinction for a half century or more, and it was one of the first endangered species to have great numbers of dedicated individuals and organizations working in its behalf. Former Secretary of the Interior Stewart Udall has described and explained these activities as ". . . a love affair between a civilized sophisticated Nation and an enormous, elusive bird. We, the people who slaughtered the bison and exterminated the passenger pigeon, have had a shift of conscience in the last fifty years and have made the preservation of rare species of wildlife one of our national conservation purposes." Because of these efforts— and also because of the bird's own vitality in the face of many odds—the fortunes of the whooping crane have improved

14

greatly in recent years. Now there is real hope for its survival. But the situation was not always so.

Decline of the Whooping Crane

In Colonial days the whooping crane was found over much of North America. It wintered from the Carolinas and Florida to the Texas Gulf Coast, and it nested across much of the Midwest and southern Canada. Carolus Linnaeus, the inventor of our modern system of scientific classification, first described and named the bird from two specimens, one taken in the Carolinas, the other in the Hudson Bay region of Canada.

Probably never numerous, the whooping crane numbered perhaps 1500 to 2000 birds in the early nineteenth century when John James Audubon, the noted naturalist and bird artist, observed their feeding activities and courtship behavior and was excited by their trumpeting call. In Audubon's time the species nested in the broad sweep of prairie marshlands from Illinois to Minnesota, the Dakotas, and the southern prairie provinces of Canada. As the land became more settled and cultivated, the only whooping crane populations that survived were those that were located away from human activities. The old territories in the states had become too populated, and the marshes the cranes needed were being drained for agricultural crops.

The numbers of whooping cranes declined steadily as this traditional nesting habitat was lost. Also, many of the big white birds fell to gunners while making their long migration flights between the northern breeding grounds and southern wintering areas. Perhaps 1000 whoopers still made the twice-yearly flights a century ago, but by 1900 there were probably no more than 200 birds left. Twelve years afterward, ornithologists made a rough count of birds during migration and estimated that perhaps eighty-eight whoopers survived.

By this time the cranes had long since abandoned their old breeding grounds in the United States and relocated in wilderness areas to the north. In 1922, a nest was discovered in a remote area of Saskatchewan, the last such found for the next thirty years and more. After that find, no one knew where the cranes went when they flew north each spring.

By 1938, there were no more than twenty-nine whooping cranes left in the world, and their future looked very dim. One small migrating flock—eighteen of them in the fall of 1938—regularly wintered on the Blackjack Peninsula and surrounding coastal areas at the mouth of the San Antonio River, some fifty miles north of Corpus Christi, Texas. Fortunately for the cranes, 47,000 acres of this area had been set aside the year before as the Aransas National Wildlife Refuge, thus giving them protection along with ducks and geese.

The other flock of whooping cranes was a small group of nonmigratory birds that lived near White Lake, in the bayou country of southern Louisiana. Eleven cranes were observed there in 1938. After Hurricane Betsy in 1940, however, only six remained. One, a bird with a crippled wing, was captured in 1941 and taken to the Audubon Park Zoo in New Orleans. Named Josephine, she later attained fame as the first captive whooping crane to breed and successfully raise young. The remaining five birds around White Lake disappeared, one by one, during the next few years, until there was just one lone survivor. It was captured in 1950 and taken to Aransas.

courting whooping crane

Whooping cranes had wintered at Aransas for generations, but even after the area was established as a wildlife refuge, the birds faced many disturbances there. Great dredges, operated by the Army Corps of Engineers, made their way through crane territory, charting and clearing the Gulf Intercoastal Waterway. There was oil drilling and production on the refuge, and the Air Force regularly conducted bombing practice on nearby Matagorda Island. All these activities threatened the well-being of the birds and displaced them from some of their feeding areas. The winter census of 1941–1942 counted only fifteen birds at Aransas—thirteen adults and two young. This number was an all-time low and was especially disturbing because the tiny Louisiana flock was also rapidly dwindling.

A Cooperative Whooping Crane Project

Greatly concerned, the National Audubon Society and the Fish and Wildlife Service joined forces in 1945 to form a Cooperative Whooping Crane Project aimed at saving the surviving birds. The next year the Society sent its research director, Robert P. Allen, to Aransas to study the birds on their wintering grounds and try to determine what could be done to help them.

Allen roamed tirelessly over the refuge, observing the birds' movements, their behavior, and their feeding habits. He mapped out fourteen different areas of about 400 acres each that different crane families used as feeding territories. In 1947, and again in 1948, he traveled to the Canadian north country in a futile effort to try to solve the mystery of where the whooping cranes nested.

In 1948, the director of the Audubon Park Zoo in New Orleans, George Douglass, was persuaded to send his female whooping crane, Josephine, to Aransas for a breeding experiment. Released into a 250-acre enclosure at the refuge, Josephine was joined by Pete, a male crane that had been crippled in 1936, then rescued and kept as a pet by a Nebraska gun club. Bob Allen kept a close watch over the two birds, and in the spring of 1949, much to his delight, he discovered that Josephine had laid two eggs. His delight changed to gloom, however, when the two eggs were smashed by the cranes after twenty-four days of incubation. Two months later the ill-starred Pete died of unknown causes.

That same fall, refuge personnel at Aransas captured a wild male with a crippled wing and put it in the same enclosure with Josephine. The new male, Crip, got along well with her, and, in 1950, the two nested and became the parents of the first whooping crane ever born in captivity. The elated Allen nicknamed the historic youngster Rusty. But once more elation turned to ashes when Rusty disappeared after several days, the probable victim of a marauding raccoon or owl.

Josephine and Crip nested again the next spring, but floodwaters destroyed the nest and eggs this time. That December, director George Douglass demanded that Josephine be returned to the New Orleans zoo. The United States Department of the Interior reluctantly let her go, and sent Crip along so the pair would not be split up.

Discovery of the Nesting Grounds

The free-flying wild cranes at Aransas were also having their ups and downs during the period that Allen was watching them. From the low of fifteen birds in the winter of 1941–1942, the flock increased to thirty-four birds by the fall of 1949. Three years later, the total had dwindled to twenty-one birds. Twenty-one birds flew north in the spring of 1955, but a total of twenty-eight—including eight young —came back that fall. The fortunes of the wild whoopers seemed to be looking up once again. The crane's migration routes in the United States had been pretty well mapped by this time, and the Audubon Society had conducted intensive publicity campaigns to educate people along the route to recognize the cranes and protect them.

Meanwhile, Allen had been searching for the unknown nesting grounds and had logged many thousands of miles flying over Canadian subarctic regions with the hope of spotting the elusive birds on their breeding territory. During World War II, while Allen was in the Army, other ornithologists—including Fred Bard, Jr., Curator of the Provincial Museum of Natural History at Regina, Saskatchewan, Fish and Wildlife biologist Bob Smith, and Olin Sewall Pettingill, Jr.—continued the search, crisscrossing Alberta, Saskatchewan, and the Yukon Territory, all to no avail. Back at work, Allen came close to a solution of the mystery in 1947, when his plane was scheduled to search Wood Buffalo National Park, which lay on the border of Alberta and the Northwest Territories, and just to the south of Great Slave Lake. Bad weather, however, forced his plane to land at a small government outpost, Fort Smith. The next year Allen extended his search into Arctic Canada, traveling 15,000 miles in a small plane. Once again, nothing.

The big break came six years later, on June 20, 1954, when a helicopter was sent out from Fort Smith to fight a fire in one section of Wood Buffalo Park, and the pilot spotted a pair of whoopers and a chick. It was too late in the season for Allen to follow the lead that year, but in April, 1955, when a Canadian wildlife biologist in a plane spotted and photographed a pair of cranes, Allen promptly headed north. The mystery of the nesting grounds was solved at last, and Allen was determined to study the whooping crane at first hand on its far northern breeding grounds.

After several false starts and more than a month of hardship and frustration as he struggled to reach the right spot in the muskeg wilderness, Allen finally set up camp close to nesting whoopers. He was in an almost impenetrable section of Wood Buffalo National Park, a remote area of bogs and ponds, winding streams, open marshes, and forests of spruce and tamarack. He spent ten days in this wilderness and gathered detailed data on the nesting habitat and the many plants and animals that shared the area with the whooping cranes.

Notes taken, Allen headed for home, satisfied at last that he had gotten the information he needed about the whooping crane's requirements on its nesting grounds as well as on its winter territory in Texas. Now everyone concerned could direct their main efforts toward putting this vital information to work in a program to help preserve the species in the wild.

There were some people, however, who thought that the main preservation effort should be directed toward breeding the species in captivity. This view was one that would stir up a great deal of controversy in the years to come.

Josephine and Crip

After they were taken from Aransas in December, 1951, the captive cranes Josephine and Crip settled into life in a small enclosure at the Audubon Park Zoo in New Orleans. For several years they showed little evidence of breeding. But in the spring of 1955, about the same time Robert Allen was exploring the northern nesting grounds, Josephine laid two eggs. Unfortunately, both of them were smashed by the birds during the excitement of a prematurely called press conference.

In 1956, Josephine laid two more eggs, both of which hatched. One downy youngster disappeared when it was just a couple of days old, the possible victim of a rat or owl. The other one grew and flourished, and excitement ran high. Success seemed at hand. After six weeks, however, the second chick sickened and died. An autopsy showed that it had succumbed to aspergillosus, a lung disease common to chickens. Although breeding whooping cranes in captivity now seemed a distinct possibility, it had not yet been done successfully.

The National Audubon Society was still firmly convinced that the only way to preserve the species was to protect and help it in the wild. Just the opposite view was held by a determined group of aviculturists, people who breed and rear birds in captivity. The procedure that they advocated was to capture some of the wild birds and start a captive breeding flock. Afterward a way probably could be found to return some of the offspring to the wild. At the very least, the species would survive in captivity.

Pressured by these two opposing groups, the Fish and Wildlife Service called representatives of both sides together in the fall of 1956. As a result of that meeting a Whooping Crane Advisory Group was formed with each point of view represented. The group was directed to review the entire situation and recommend the best program to help the cranes.

When the breeding season of 1957 arrived, Josephine laid eggs as usual; this time they received expert human attention. George Scott, the Head Keeper of Birds at the New York Zoological Park, who had many years of experience raising birds in captivity, was sent to New Orleans to supervise and oversee operations. With Scott's help, Josephine and Crip successfully raised two young that year. They were duly named George and Georgette, in honor of George Douglass, Director of the Audubon Park Zoo, and George Scott of the Bronx Zoo.

In 1958, Josephine and Crip raised another youngster, which was named Pepper, and it provided another positive argument for those who advocated raising whooping cranes in captivity. The wild whoopers also raised nine young in Canada that summer and brought them all back to Aransas in the fall. This yearly increase was the greatest so far. The wild flock now totaled thirty-two birds.

In 1959, Josephine once again laid two eggs, but promptly smashed them. George Scott was quickly summoned, and Josephine obligingly laid five more eggs. They were placed in an incubator, but none of them hatched. Evidently only two had been fertile.

That same year a Whooping Crane Conservation Association, dedicated to captive breeding of the species, was formed. As if to bolster the hopes of the association members, Josephine raised her fourth youngster, Peewee, in 1961.

All in all, the valiant Josephine laid more than fifty eggs during a long life in captivity. But only four of them resulted in young that were raised successfully. In September, 1965, Josephine's life came to an end, just after Hurricane Betsy had passed through New Orleans. She survived the storm satisfactorily, but in its aftermath was frightened by a low-flying helicopter and flew into her fence with great force. Her mate, Crip, was then paired with Rosie, another wing-crippled female crane that had been sent to Audubon Park from the San Antonio Zoo just the year before. Eventually, both Rosie and Crip were sent back to the San Antonio Zoo.

The Endangered Species Program

The numbers of the wild flock at Aransas fluctuated from year to year, but the total continued to edge upward slowly, thanks in part to the ongoing program of public education about the birds and increased concern about their plight. In the fall of 1964 there were forty-two birds in the flock, a new high. Ten of them were youngsters that had hatched in Canada that summer. Another young bird that had been injured in Canada was captured and brought to the Monte Vista Wildlife Refuge in Colorado. It was named Canus, after Canada and the United States.

A number of captive sandhill cranes were at Monte Vista also. They were being studied and bred in captivity in a pilot program initiated several years before by Dr. Ray C. Erickson, a veteran wildlife biologist with the United States Fish and Wildlife Service. As a member of the Service's Division of Wildlife Research, Erickson had formulated a three-pronged plan for helping endangered species. The plan combined extensive field studies and laboratory research with a program of captive propagation of the species and a later release of captive-bred specimens to the wild. Before any serious attempt would be made to raise a captive flock of any endangered bird, however, Erickson thought that a great deal of valuable experience and information could be gained by raising common relatives of the threatened species, such as sandhill cranes. In 1961, his plan was put into practice on a very modest scale at Monte Vista, with the building of a few temporary sandhill crane enclosures.

In the meantime, with the wild flock of whoopers grow-

24

ing in size, Fish and Wildlife personnel at Aransas began an experimental program of putting out supplementary grain for the birds. Most of the crane population began to gather at the feeding station, and the program was discontinued because of the possibility of the transmission of disease from one bird to the whole flock.

The increasing prominence of the cranes as symbols of the efforts of wildlife conservation helped the species to turn back several new threats. One was a proposed railroad through the Canadian nesting territory, which was rerouted after public outcry. Another was a plan of the United States Air Force to use Matagorda Island, next door to Aransas, for photoflash bombing. This project, too, was cancelled after a similar outcry.

Important developments in the continuing struggle to save the whooping crane now began to emerge in rapid succession, thanks in part to Erickson's ideas. In June, 1964, the United States Department of the Interior and the Canadian Wildlife Service jointly announced plans to remove whooping crane eggs from wild nests sometime within the next several years and begin a program of rearing the cranes in captivity. A few months later, Secretary of the Interior Stewart L. Udall announced the start of a new endangered-species program that would be carried out under the auspices of the Fish and Wildlife Service. Early in 1965, urged on by staunch conservationist Karl Mundt, senator from South Dakota, Congress voted $350,000 to initiate the Endangered Wildlife Research Program at Patuxent Wildlife Research Center in Laurel, Maryland. Erickson was appointed Assistant Director for Endangered Wildlife Research at Patuxent, and whooping cranes were high on his agenda.

In February, 1966, Canus was sent from Monte Vista to

Patuxent, and so were a number of sandhill cranes. These near relatives would continue their role as stand-ins for whoopers in the developing research program.

Operation Egg Hunt

The initial stages of Operation Egg Hunt were carried out in June, 1967, when Canadian wildlife officials located the nests of six pairs of whoopers in Wood Buffalo Park and removed an egg from each. The six eggs were flown to Patuxent in padded suitcase incubators developed at the research center. One of the eggs hatched during the flight and the chick died, unable to stand the rarefied atmosphere at high altitudes. The other five eggs were placed in an incubator where they hatched. The young were cared for by keepers clothed in white, their faces masked, in order to prevent the possibility of the chicks being imprinted with human beings—becoming conditioned to following their keepers as their natural parents.

This ambitious and controversial program of collecting Canadian eggs had been under consideration for several years. The National Audubon Society had at first opposed the idea, for it believed that even if cranes could be bred and raised in captivity, the possibility of successfully returning the young to the wild was remote. And merely maintaining a captive population, in the opinion of some conservationists, was hardly better than keeping a flock of chickens.

Erickson, however, thought that captive-bred cranes could eventually be returned to the wild. He also asserted that the captive program would not endanger or reduce the wild flock. If one egg was taken from a wild crane, he noted, the female would lay another. Indeed, the captive

Josephine had laid seven eggs in 1959 when one egg after another had been taken from her in the New Orleans zoo. Taking eggs from the nests—as five years of experimentation with wild sandhill cranes had shown—should in no way affect the number of young raised in the wild.

Events seemed to bear out Erickson's arguments. That fall thirty-eight wild whoopers accompanied by nine young, a total of forty-seven, arrived at Aransas. The taking of six eggs the preceding spring had evidently not adversely affected the nesting of the wild birds. While the normal clutch in the wild is two, most pairs of whooping cranes raise no more than one young each season.

In the spring of 1968, ten eggs were gathered in Canada and transported to Patuxent. Nine of them hatched. At the same time, Rosie and Crip laid five eggs at the San Antonio Zoo. The year before they had raised one young bird, Tex, which had been sent to Patuxent. In the fall of 1968 there was a grand total of sixty-seven whooping cranes in the world.

Between 1967 and 1974, Operation Egg Hunt yielded fifty eggs and one chick in five different pickups for Patuxent. Twenty cranes that hatched from these eggs were raised successfully, and were still living in 1974. The first breeding attempts of the Patuxent flock showed definite promise, too. A few eggs had already been produced by the captive-reared cranes, but not until 1975 did a second-generation captive crane hatch successfully. Named Dawn, the whooper chick lived only several days. But, as its name suggests, the mere fact of its hatching raised hopes for the future. Two pairs of captive cranes laid eggs the next year. From them, one second-generation youngster was successfully reared. In 1978, three more were reared.

Sandhill Cranes as Foster Parents

The year 1975 was also the time that an ambitious foster-parent plan for whooping crane eggs and chicks was put into effect. The plan was simply to take eggs from wild nests in Canada as before, but instead of sending them to incubators at Patuxent, they would be flown directly to Idaho. There, on the Grays Lake National Wildlife Refuge, they would be placed in the nests of wild greater sandhill cranes, from which the natural eggs had been removed.

Accordingly, in early June, fourteen Canadian eggs were placed in Idaho nests, and nine of them hatched under their foster parents.

Dr. Rod Drewien of the University of Idaho's Cooperative Wildlife Research Unit observed the progress of the young whoopers and their parents all that summer. In August, all but one of the young flightless whooping cranes were captured, banded, and color marked. That fall Drewien, driving a pickup truck, accompanied the sandhill cranes and the six young whoopers that had survived to flight stage as they started their migration from Idaho to their regular wintering grounds on the Bosque del Apache National Wildlife Refuge in New Mexico.

A second flock of wild whooping cranes seemed to be in the making. Whether the whoopers hatched at Gray's Lake would establish a regular migratory route for themselves between Idaho and New Mexico, and whether they would breed among themselves when they matured or attempt to mate with sandhill cranes, were questions that still remained to be answered.

The Population Increases

During that same summer of 1975, eight young whoopers were raised by their natural parents in Canada. By De-

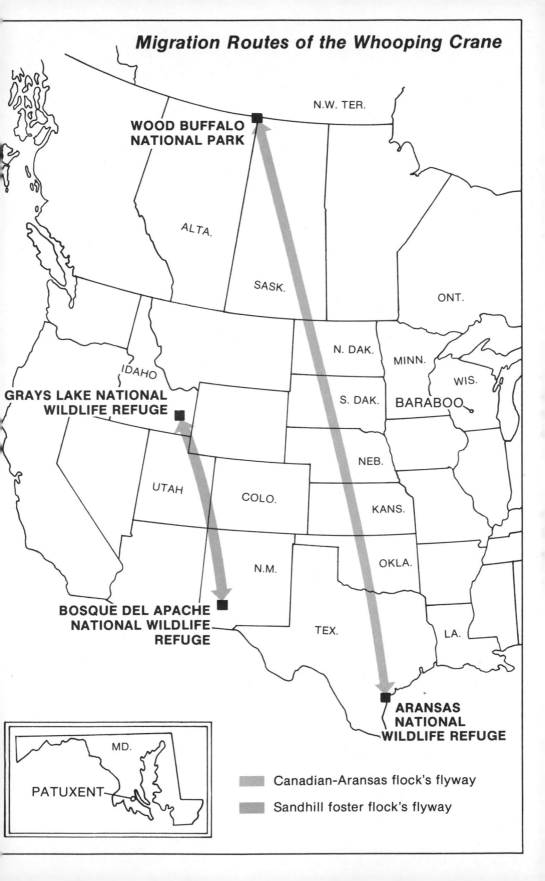

Migration Routes of the Whooping Crane

N.W. TER.

WOOD BUFFALO
NATIONAL PARK

ALTA.

SASK.

ONT.

IDAHO

N. DAK.

MINN.

WIS.

GRAYS LAKE NATIONAL
WILDLIFE REFUGE

S. DAK.

BARABOO

UTAH

COLO.

NEB.

KANS.

N.M.

OKLA.

BOSQUE DEL APACHE
NATIONAL WILDLIFE
REFUGE

TEX.

LA.

ARANSAS
NATIONAL
WILDLIFE REFUGE

MD.

PATUXENT

Canadian-Aransas flock's flyway

Sandhill foster flock's flyway

cember, the world population of the big white birds, wild and captive, stood at a new high of eighty-three.

In 1976, a total of fifteen Canadian eggs were transplanted to sandhill crane nests in Idaho. Eleven of them hatched, but coyotes and summer storms took a high toll. Seven young Idaho whoopers—young of the year and yearlings—were counted in the fall. The Canadian cranes produced a total of thirty-two eggs that same year, and twelve chicks migrated to Aransas with their parents. At Patuxent, two pairs of captive whoopers produced three eggs after artificial insemination. One of them hatched, but the young crane died before it could grow up. The official world population of whooping cranes that winter was ninety-nine individuals, counting all the Aransas birds, the emerging Bosque del Apache flock, and nineteen captive cranes.

On June 24, 1977, elated Fish and Wildlife officials announced that twenty-nine whooping cranes had hatched that spring, bringing the total population to a possible one hundred twenty-six whooping cranes. The flock of sixty-nine wild Aransas birds had produced thirty-four eggs on their Canadian breeding grounds; sixteen of them had been sent to Grays Lake. The nineteen captive birds at Patuxent had produced twenty-two eggs, and fourteen of them had also been sent to Idaho. There were at least eleven young in Canada, and twelve had hatched at Grays Lake. The remaining eggs incubated at Patuxent had produced two second-generation chicks, and another egg was being incubated there by a pair of sandhill cranes.

Drought hit the sandhill nesting grounds in Idaho later that summer, and most of the young whoopers that had just hatched there were lost. Indeed, losses of young Idaho whooping cranes to drought, storms, and predators had been unexpectedly high over the first three years of the program. But in spite of the setbacks, a new flock was definitely in the making at Grays Lake. Best of all, whooping cranes in general seemed to have passed the critical point in numbers. A parade of new developments augured well for the future, and many different people in different places were working in the cranes' behalf.

New Developments and Techniques

Not the least of these people were two young graduates of Cornell University, George Archibald and Ronald Sauey. In the spring of 1973 they established the International Crane Foundation at Baraboo, Wisconsin. Their goal: "the conservation of the world's cranes through research, habitat protection, captive breeding, restocking, and public education." At present, all except one of the fifteen different species of cranes in the world are being studied on the foundation's grounds. A number of them are regularly breeding there.

In the spring of 1976, Archibald and Sauey received their first two whooping cranes, one a male survivor of the New Orleans zoo flock, another a female hatched at the San Antonio Zoo and reared at Patuxent. The next year they received a second male whooper from Patuxent.

A number of innovative and effective methods for determining the sex, breeding, and raising cranes in captivity have been developed by Archibald and Sauey. Many species are bred through artificial insemination, a procedure perfected at Patuxent by Dr. George F. Gee, a research physiologist. Since male and female cranes of most species are almost impossible to tell apart in the wild except through their behavior or dominance patterns, Archibald and Sauey, as well as the scientists at Patuxent and elsewhere, have experimented with several rather sophisticated methods of

sexing cranes. Internal examination of the cloaca is one of the older methods used. Several other methods now being studied include chromosome analysis of a drop of crane blood and analysis of sex steroids found in waste materials. Any of the above techniques necessitate the capture and handling of the birds. But one of the easiest and most effective methods of sexing cranes is to listen to the individual bird's calls, which are distinct for each sex, during the breeding season, and to observe each bird's courtship behavior. This method was perfected at Baraboo.

At Patuxent, young whooping cranes are raised with turkey or sandhill chicks so that the whooping crane chicks' hostility to one another, which sometimes ends in injuries, can be dispersed. When they are old enough, prospective pairs are separated into spacious and isolated breeding pens. Recently, floodlights have been used in the springtime to lengthen the hours of daylight gradually and simulate natural conditions at the Canadian nesting grounds. When the wild cranes are breeding, almost twenty-two hours out of each twenty-four are daylight.

Although great strides are being made in raising whooping cranes in captivity, the final step—the technique of releasing captive-raised whooping cranes into the wild—has not yet been fully worked out. One possibility is to keep the young until they are a year old, for the greatest losses of young cranes come during that critical first year in the wild. Yearlings would then be released during their second summer in the vicinity of a wild flock of whooping cranes or sandhills with the hope that with the arrival of fall they would follow the wild birds on their southward migration. Nine different areas on the cranes' migration routes were

whooping crane chicks

established as critical habitat in 1978, and eight other such areas have been proposed. The designation of these critical habitats will give the whooping cranes greater protection on their long flights to and from their nesting grounds.

In the fall of 1978, a total of seventy-four wild cranes—including six young—made the flight south from Canada to the wintering grounds at Aransas. Another nine free-flying whoopers were counted in the emerging Rocky Mountain flock—birds hatched in Grays Lake, Idaho. Counting both wild and captive birds, the total whooping crane population stood at one hundred nine specimens in the winter of 1978-1979.

In November, 1975, the Fish and Wildlife Service, as it had done for a number of other endangered species, appointed a Whooping Crane Recovery Team, with David L. Olsen of the Service's Refuge Division as its Team Leader. The team was charged with drawing up recovery plans and overseeing programs for improving the future status of the big birds. In December, 1978, the recovery team issued a review draft of its recovery plan for the species. Two important features of the plan were the proposal to increase the Wood Buffalo-Aransas population to a minimum of forty pairs, and the establishment of at least two additional populations, with a minimum of twenty nesting pairs each. The nine whooping cranes hatched at Grays Lake are at least a start toward one of those flocks. A difficulty that any new flock will face is the limited suitable habitat still available for winter territory.

At Patuxent, Ray Erickson's staff ponders the plans for establishing other foster-parent flocks. A favored proposal is the use of a flock of greater sandhill cranes that breed in Manitoba, Ontario, or Minnesota, and winter in Florida.

2

THE BALD EAGLE, AMERICA'S NATIONAL BIRD

2084716

After hovering for a moment some twenty feet above the surface of the lake, an osprey plunges downward and splashes into the water. Rising, it clutches a foot-long fish, a carp, in its talons. The fish hawk has captured a meal for its young. Its long, narrow wings beating strongly, the osprey heads for its nest in a dead tree across the lake.

A bald eagle, soaring high above, spots the successful hunter. Plunging with half-closed wings, the great bird of prey dives at the fish hawk and screams a warning: *kark-kark-kark-kark!* The osprey dodges and avoids the attack, but the eagle quickly circles back and swoops at the smaller bird once again. The osprey changes course a second time in its effort to escape. Back comes the relentless eagle, so close this time that its wings brush those of the osprey. The fish hawk gives up. It drops the fish and retreats.

Diving, the bald eagle seizes the carp before it reaches the water and carries it to the nearest shore, where it lands to eat its prize. The robber's fierce eyes are yellow. So is the strong, hooked beak that tears at the white flesh of the fish. Every movement of the great bird of prey conveys power and arrogance.

Eagles have been used as symbols of imperial power since ancient times and were featured in the pageantry of many

bald eagle with prey

conquerors, from Caesar to Kaiser Wilhelm. In the United States, however, the eagle was chosen as a symbol of freedom when it was adopted as the national bird in 1782. While most citizens of the new nation hailed the choice, Benjamin Franklin voiced objections. He did not think well of the eagle at all. Instead, he favored the turkey, claiming that it was a more useful and fully American bird. "I wish the bald eagle had not been chosen as the representative of our country," he wrote to his niece. "He is a bird of bad moral character; he does not get his living honestly." Franklin referred to the bald eagle's habit of often robbing an osprey of its catch.

While Americans took Franklin's advice on many subjects, they disregarded his opinion about the bald eagle as the official emblem of the country. It was soon featured on coins and on the great seal of the United States, as well as on many heraldric devices and insignia.

Fish are the mainstay of the bald eagle's diet, but it may take other small animals of many kinds on occasion. Eagles also feed on deer and other animal carcasses. Probably this fact was what caused John James Audubon to echo Franklin about the bald eagle's character. In his bird biographies, Audubon could not resist concluding his account of the species with the following: ". . . suffer me, kind reader, to say how much I grieve that it should have been selected as the Emblem of my Country. The opinion of our great Franklin on this subject . . . perfectly coincides with my own. . . ."

In those early days of the republic, the bald eagle—it was also called the American eagle, or the white-headed eagle —ranged throughout most of North America, from Alaska to northern Mexico.

The Eagle's Life-style

An adult eagle measures about two and a half feet from beak to tip of tail and weighs eight to twelve pounds. Its broad wings in flight measure six or seven feet from tip to tip. The adult plumage is deep, dusky brown, except for the white head and tail. Immature bald eagles, as large as their parents or slightly larger, are dark all over except for their light wing linings. They are often mistaken for adult golden eagles. The latter birds are darker, however, and do not have the whitish wing linings. Audubon evidently found the young bald eagles far more impressive birds than the adults. In 1815, he shot an immature specimen and was convinced that it was a new species. Naming it the Bird of Washington, he claimed that ". . . it is indisputably the noblest bird of its genus that has yet been discovered in the United States."

Immature birds take four or five years to gain the white head and tail of adulthood and to be ready to mate. Bald eagles mate for life and may live thirty or forty years or more. Under good conditions, a pair may raise one to three young each year.

The same nest is used year after year. Each spring the adult birds add a few sticks or branches to the bulky structure, which is usually built high in the crown of a lofty tree. Sometimes the nest reaches huge proportions. Dr. Francis Herrick, a biologist at Western Reserve University, studied an immense nest near Vermillion, Ohio, a half century ago. It measured eight and a half feet in diameter, was twelve feet thick, and was thought to weigh at least two tons.

Dr. Herrick was the first man to study the bald eagle's life history in detail. In order to observe the Vermillion eagles, he built a platform in an elm tree close to their nest and watched the birds from a blind he erected on it. Unfortunately, a storm soon brought down both the tree and nest, carrying three young eagles with it. When the pair had rebuilt in another location, the persistent Herrick had his tower moved as well. At the same time he increased its height to ninety feet, so he could look down and watch every move of the nesting birds.

Decline of the Bald Eagle

In Herrick's day the eagle was still a fairly common bird in the forty-eight states, especially on both coasts, around the Great Lakes, and along principal waterways. In the Territory of Alaska it was abundant. Salmon fishermen disliked the big birds, for they fed on salmon that the fishermen thought were rightfully theirs. From 1917 to 1952, the Territory offered a bounty of two dollars for every eagle killed, and in those thirty-five years made bounty payments on 128,273 Alaskan eagles.

The average size of Alaskan eagles, as well as those of Canada and the Northern states, is slightly larger than those found further south. On that basis, ornithologists have rather arbitrarily separated the species into two races, considering those that nest north of the fortieth parallel northern bald eagles and those nesting south of it southern bald eagles.

Today the bald eagle remains a common bird in Alaska. Its population in the forty-eight states below Canada, however, has dwindled drastically in the past fifty years. A number of factors have contributed to the decline. Lumbering operations have destroyed many eagle-nest trees over the years, and land clearing and development have eliminated much suitable eagle habitat. When roads, houses, or other structures are built too close to nesting areas, or if the birds are unduly disturbed by human activities of any kind, they often abandon their nests. Many eagles, along with all other birds of prey, still fall victim to gunners, especially in several Western states where sheep ranchers blame both golden and bald eagles for killing lambs. Many eagles have also died from poisoned baits put out in Federal or state pest-and-predator-control projects.

Even more insidious, however, has been the eagles' consumption of fish and other animals that carry concentrations of DDT and other long-lived pesticides in their body. These chlorinated-hydrocarbon pesticides were not used widely in the United States until after World War II, but many scientists suspected at the time (the 1950s and early 1960s) that they were affecting the reproduction of eagles and other birds of prey. Years of research finally proved that they were right in their suspicions.

Concerned about the eagle's decline south of Alaska, the Federal Government in 1948 extended full protection to the species in the 48 lower states, with a penalty of a five hundred dollar fine and/or a six-month jail sentence for killing a bald eagle. The Territory of Alaska was exempted from the ban, however, and the bounty there remained in effect for another four years. It was discontinued in 1952, when the territorial legislature extended protection to the Alaskan bald eagles as well.

The Eagle Man

Florida has always been a stronghold of the southern bald eagle, and the decline of the species in that state during the 1940s and 1950s was especially alarming. The dwindling population and the drastic reduction in breeding success in the Sunshine State were vividly demonstrated

40

by the records compiled by Charles L. Broley, a retired businessman who banded young eagles for the Fish and Wildlife Service as a hobby. Enthusiastic and tireless, Broley was known far and wide as the Eagle Man. During his lifetime he banded more than 1200 young eagles, a record that should stand for a long time. Climbing up to eaglets in their lofty nest, then banding them with an aluminum band while fending off their sharp beaks and claws, not to mention the anxious parents, is no easy task. Records of attacks on a bander by the parent birds are quite rare, but they have happened.

After locating an eagle nest and determining that it contained eaglets, Broley would set to work. Using a slingshot to get a fishing line over a high limb, he followed up with a clothesline, and then a one-inch rope. He used this rope for support as he made his way up to a spot where he could fasten a hooked iron rod into the nest and secure it. Climbing into the eagle's eyrie, Broley would then fasten a heavy aluminum band to the left foot of each hissing youngster. The later recovery of eagles with such bands helps to determine migration routes, longevity, and other facts of eagle life.

In 1946, Broley banded about one hundred fifty eaglets in Florida. In 1950, just four years later, he noted that only 22 percent of his long-observed eagle nests had young in them; that year he was able to band only twenty-one young birds. For some reason, the adult birds were failing to nest successfully. In 1955, Broley found only eight young eagles in his usual Florida territory, and by 1958 just one. Broley died the next year, but his work had demonstrated beyond doubt that something was terribly wrong with eagle reproduction in Florida.

The same fate, furthermore, seemed to be overtaking

other birds of prey, such as the osprey and the peregrine falcon. Were organic pesticides, as many scientists suspected, the cause of this reproductive failure?

Rachel Carson warned of the consequences of unrestricted use of such poisons in her 1962 book, *Silent Spring*. Her findings were bitterly debated across the country, as many scientists hastened to try to find out more information about DDT and its related hydrocarbon poisons.

The Effect of Pesticides on Wildlife

The Fish and Wildlife Service had begun to study the effects of DDT on wildlife as long ago as 1945, and in the early 1950s a federal biologist, James B. DeWitt, demonstrated that a low but steady intake of DDT did indeed affect the reproductive success of game birds.

From 1956 to 1958, DDT was spread widely across the Northeast in an attempt to stop the spread of the gypsy moth. At the same time, the Department of Agriculture was blanketing much of the South with chlorinated hydrocarbons in a similar campaign to wipe out the fire ant. In Michigan, Dr. George Wallace, a biologist at Michigan State University, was documenting the deadly effect on songbirds when DDT was used to combat the spread of Dutch elm disease. Wallace predicted that unless the use of such pesticides was curbed, "We shall have been witness, within a single decade, to a greater extermination of animal life than in all the previous years of man's history on earth."

Additional research showed that DDT used for mosquito control in Clear Lake, California, was killing grebes and other water birds. Sprayed over the lake, the pesticide was taken in along with food by tiny aquatic creatures such as mosquito and other insect larvae and stored in their bodies. They were eaten in turn by minnows and amphibians, which were swallowed by larger amphibians and fish. With each step the poisons accumulated in ever more concentrated doses in the animals' tissues. Finally the fish were eaten by grebes and other fish-eating birds, with disastrous consequences. Unlike the grebes, eagles were not killed outright by DDT. They just failed to reproduce normally.

Alarmed by the bald eagle's decline, the National Audubon Society set out to investigate its status throughout North America. As a first step in Audubon's Continental Bald Eagle Project, Alexander Sprunt IV, the Society's Research Director since the death of Bob Allen, inaugurated a nationwide census of bald eagles in the forty-eight lower states. Fish and Wildlife personnel, staff members of many state fish-and-game departments, local Audubon Society members, and many interested individuals all helped in the count. Conducted in January, 1961, the census added up to a total of 3576 eagles. Since this first count, others have been taken yearly. Today they are usually conducted under the supervision of the Fish and Wildlife Service. Spotting the big birds from aircraft, the census takers count both nesting pairs and their young.

As the 1960s rolled on, the evidence of serious nesting failure among the eagles increased, and the case against DDT as a principal cause of the failure strengthened. A study of fifty-eight eagle carcasses at the Patuxent Wildlife Research Center showed that all but one contained pesticide residues. Three of the nation's most respected wildlife ornithologists—Roger Tory Peterson, Roland Clement of the National Audubon Society, and Joseph Hickey of the University of Wisconsin—sounded an alarm against the continued use of such poisons. The public in general was being

overleaf: bald eagles

alerted to the dangers of organic pesticides and to the serious trouble they were causing a number of birds such as the osprey, peregrine falcon, and bald eagle.

Protecting the Bald Eagle

As the evidence of nesting failure among eagles increased in the 1960s, many groups and individuals came forward to help our national bird. Through a program sponsored by local Audubon societies, some 1,678,000 acres of Florida land had been designated as eagle sanctuaries by 1964. About half of the active nests in the state were on this protected land.

In 1966, Secretary of the Interior Stewart Udall took several important steps to help protect eagles from human disturbance. Nesting sites in national wildlife refuges were closed to human trespass, with no cutting of timber permitted within a half mile. The eagle was classified as rare in the Southeastern states, where a 1963 survey had showed just 230 active nests. By this time, the Florida Audubon Society had reached agreement with landowners to set aside 2,300,000 acres of land as eagle sanctuaries. The next year the Fish and Wildlife Service designated the southern bald eagle an endangered species.

Many groups of people in other areas were also doing their part to help. The Northern States Power Company of Minneapolis, for example, took steps to protect eagles and their nests on some 30,000 acres of land it controlled along the Saint Croix River in Minnesota and Wisconsin—prime eagle nesting territory; the Red Lake band of Chippewa Indians in Minnesota designated its 400,000 acre reservation an eagle sanctuary; and the Weyerhaeuser Company posted regulations to protect eagles in its timber holdings in Washington and Oregon. In 1968, two Federal agencies—the Fish and Wildlife Service and the Forest Service—reached general agreement to protect eagle-nest trees and young from disturbance in southeastern Alaska. There were still many eagles in our far Northern state, but the census in the lower forty-eight that year counted only 2772 eagles.

Hard evidence of the effect of DDT on the reproduction of eagles, pelicans, and many other birds began to surface in the late 1960s. Experiments at Patuxent clearly demonstrated that DDT fed to captive sparrow hawks and mallard ducks hindered successful reproduction. Even a very little amount of DDE—a breakdown product of DDT—caused significant thinning in the shells of mallard duck eggs. Many such thin-shelled eggs were crushed during incubation. Others contained deformed young or embryos that died during development.

DDT and Nesting Failure

One key piece of evidence convicting DDT resulted from the research of Dr. Derek Ratcliffe in England. Long concerned about the decline of peregrine falcons in his country, Ratcliffe conducted a series of experiments in 1967 on peregrine falcon eggshells. (He used museum specimens for this research.) His studies demonstrated that eggs laid before 1946, when many of the new organic pesticides had been introduced, had shells that were 20 percent heavier than shells of eggs collected at later dates. Ratcliffe sent his findings to Dr. Joseph Hickey at the University of Wisconsin. The next year Hickey duplicated the research with American eggs and confirmed Ratcliffe's findings.

In their published report, Hickey and his co-author noted the cause-and-effect relationship between the use of DDT and the subsequent eggshell thinning and reproductive failure noted among many birds species. At about this time, too, a Cornell chemist, David Peakall, showed by experimentation that DDE upsets the hormone and enzyme balance necessary in birds for normal reproduction and the production of calcium for eggshells.

All of the evidence showed that DDT and related pesticides posed a deadly threat to many wildlife species. These poisons, moreover, had been used in ever-increasing amounts all over the United States since the end of World War II. For more than twenty years they had been draining into streams and rivers and ultimately into the oceans surrounding the continent.

Facing the evidence, the Government finally restricted the use of DDT in 1969 and banned its use entirely in the United States in 1972. A great deal of damage had already been done, however. In many areas, eagles, ospreys, pelicans, and other fish-eating birds had disappeared completely.

The 1970 eagle census showed a decline in the bird's numbers throughout the lower forty-eight states. In addition to DDT and its derivatives, mercury, poured with industrial wastes into the Great Lakes and other waters, proved to be another cause of eagle deaths. This heavy metal remains for many years on lake bottoms and is picked up by fish as they forage and, in turn, by the eagles that eat those fish.

Many western eagles were also dying after eating poisoned bait put out in predator-control programs. Strychnine, cyanide, and Compound 1080 (sodium fluoracetate) were among the principal poisons being used. In addition, countless numbers of eagles were still being killed by shooting, often from helicopters, as some western ranchers waged war on all predators. Golden eagles were the usual targets, but many bald eagles were also shot. The killing of bald eagles was strictly illegal under any circumstances, and the killing of golden eagles was allowed only under special circumstances and with a special Federal permit. Convictions in cases of shooting eagles, however, were generally hard to obtain. Several Wyoming and Colorado ranchers reportedly paid as much as twenty-five dollars for each eagle shot by hunters pursuing them in helicopters. Nearly 800 eagles were reportedly killed in this manner in 1970 and 1971. As a result, the National Wildlife Federation offered a reward for information leading to conviction of eagle killers.

New Developments in Eagle Research

In 1974, the National Wildlife Federation launched a publicity campaign, Save a Living Thing, to raise money to purchase tracts of Missouri River bottomland in South Dakota that provided wintering areas for hundreds of bald eagles. The 7-Eleven Food Stores, a nationwide chain, raised and donated a considerable sum of money toward this project. In December of that year, over 1100 acres of this land were turned over to the Fish and Wildlife Service, and it became the Karl Mundt National Wildlife Refuge. This Federal refuge was the first established primarily for the protection of bald eagles.

Stepping up its eagle campaign, the National Wildlife Federation set up a computerized eagle bank at its Washington headquarters with the aim of locating all eagle nesting and roosting sites in the lower forty-eight states and protecting them from further human encroachment. "Eagles just aren't very tolerant of man," explained NWF executive vice president Thomas L. Kimball. "If they are to survive, we are going to have to make some accommodations. By collecting everything that is known about how and where they live and making it available to experts in

49

and out of government, we should be able to preserve this bird that is so much a part of the national tradition."

Science was finding new ways to help the eagles, too. Dr. Thomas J. Cade and other scientists at Cornell University's Laboratory of Ornithology had been working with captive peregrine falcons for some years. Pairs had been bred naturally or by artificial insemination, and the eggs and young were being raised under laboratory conditions. In 1972, captive golden eagles were artificially inseminated at the same laboratory, and three chicks hatched in an incubator. These young were placed in the nests of western golden eagles for raising. Such techniques would be used on various other birds of prey, including bald eagles.

In 1974, two bald eagles were removed from Wisconsin nests and transported to Maine, where they were put into the nests of native bald eagles, which had almost ceased reproducing. There had been only nineteen active eagle nests in the state the preceding year, and they had produced only seven eaglets. Four Wisconsin eggs were placed in Maine nests in 1975. The eggs that they replaced were taken to Patuxent, where they were put into incubators. Much to the surprise of many, they hatched. These eaglets were later returned to active wild nests in Maine, where they were fledged by foster parents. Census takers that year reported that thirty-three pairs of Maine bald eagles had produced fourteen young—a significant improvement over preceding years.

By this time, bald eagles had all but vanished in New York State. Just one wild breeding pair, which occupied a nest south of Rochester, was known in 1976. For five years, however, they had been unsuccessful in raising any young.

In an effort to bring bald eagles back to New York, Cornell University's Laboratory of Ornithology undertook

50

an innovative program at Montezuma National Wildlife Refuge in the central part of the state. As part of that program, a graduate student in ornithology had an unusual summer job. She lived in a tent on the refuge but spent most of her waking hours in a blind atop a thirty-five-foot tower. There she watched over and fed two young bald eagles in an artificial nest on the same platform. The eaglets had been removed from wild nests in Wisconsin and brought to Montezuma with the hope that they would stay in the area and eventually breed.

The Montezuma eaglets flourished, and were soon exercising their wings, as young birds do in their nests in the wild. By mid-July they had begun to fly; and once fledged, they left their artificial nest to explore the surrounding countryside. Each was equipped with yellow wing tags and a radio transmitter fastened to its tail, so that it could be readily identified and its movements tracked. For a while the birds returned to the tower every day for food, but in September they began catching fish for themselves in the shallow waters of the nearby lake. In mid-October they left the refuge for the winter.

This technique of feeding the birds daily until they learn how to hunt for themselves is an adaptation of a method falconers have used for centuries. Called "hacking," it involves feeding the bird at the same place or hack board daily, so that it becomes accustomed to coming back for food; at the same time, it learns how to hunt prey for itself. During this process, the bird becomes imprinted with the falconer, who becomes its surrogate parent and food provider. After further training, the bird returns even after it has learned how to kill for itself.

The aim at Montezuma, however, was to wean the birds to the wild. Therefore, the eaglets were insulated as much as possible from people so that they would not become imprinted with human beings. Those who fed and observed them were hidden in a blind close to the nest, so the young birds could not see them.

This same adaptation of the hacking technique had been used successfully the year before with peregrine falcons hatched at Cornell in its continuing program of breeding the birds in captivity and releasing them to the wild. There was good reason to believe that the method would work just as well for eagles and other birds of prey.

The next year, 1977, five young eagles were hacked at Montezuma. Two of them had hatched from eggs laid by captive eagles at Patuxent, and three from eggs taken from wild nests in Minnesota and Michigan. By August, all five had fledged successfully. Even more encouraging, one of the yearling eagles fledged the year before returned to the area. The success story continued in 1978, when four eaglets were conditioned at Montezuma and returned to the wild in the same way.

The Bald Eagle Begins to Recover

A further cause for cheer was the performance of the last remaining wild pair of New York eagles. A two-week-old eaglet, hatched from the egg of captive eagles at Patuxent, was placed in their nest that spring, and the old birds successfully raised it. With such programs, the bald eagle was starting its long way back in New York.

Pennsylvania's eagles have been in desperate straits too. In 1976, just three bald eagle nests remained, all near the Pymatuning Reservoir in Crawford County. One pair of eagles had nested in this area for over twenty years. During the last fourteen years, however, they had not succeeded in raising any young. In 1976, their huge old nesting tree

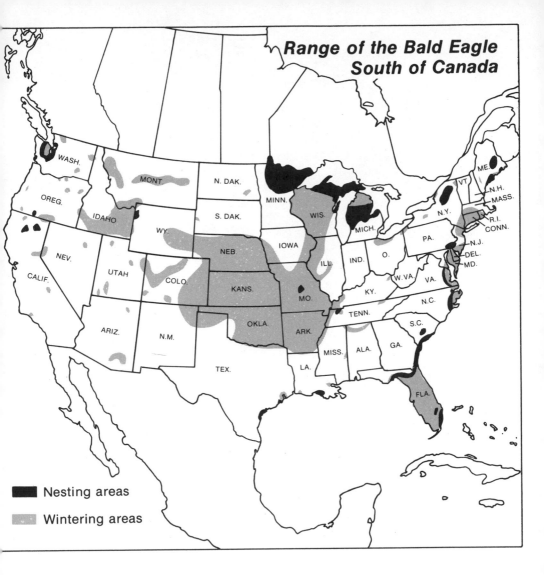

Range of the Bald Eagle South of Canada

WASH.

MONT.

N. DAK.

MINN.

ME.

VT

N.H.

MASS.

N.Y.

OREG.

IDAHO

S. DAK.

WIS.

MICH.

PA.

R.I.

CONN.

WY.

IOWA

O.

N.J.

DEL.

MD.

NEV.

UTAH

NEB.

ILL

IND.

W.VA.

VA.

CALIF.

COLO.

KANS.

MO.

KY.

N.C.

ARIZ.

N.M.

OKLA.

ARK.

TENN.

S.C.

GA.

MISS.

ALA.

TEX.

LA.

FLA.

■ Nesting areas

░ Wintering areas

was toppled by a windstorm, so wildlife biologists built an artificial nest for them in a platform placed in a dead elm tree close to the old site. Accepting their new home, the eagles laid eggs and raised two young.

Although Alaska still had an estimated 7000 or more pairs of breeding eagles (some say as many as 15,000), and Canada may support an even larger population, the 1976 census showed fewer than 4000 eagles in the forty-eight

bald eagle in flight

states below Canada. In this total were only about 700 breeding pairs, including 318 pairs in the Lake States, 150 pairs in Florida, 101 in the Pacific Northwest, 56 in the Chesapeake Bay region, 33 in Maine, and some 50 pairs scattered throughout other areas. In 1978, the Fish and Wildlife Service listed the bald eagle as endangered in forty-three of the states below Canada, and threatened in the other five states—Minnesota, Wisconsin, Michigan, Oregon, and Washington.

By this time, widespread use of DDT and its related pesticides was years in the past. In many areas, eagles were beginning, in a small but encouraging way, to reproduce successfully once more. In 1977, there were seventy-seven active eagle nests in the Chesapeake region, and a total of sixty-nine eaglets raised, the best record for the area since the 1936 eagle survey.

Eagle populations in the Upper Great Lakes region, the Pacific Northwest, and Florida all appeared to be maintaining themselves successfully too; in some areas they were even increasing. In 1978, Florida eagles actively occupied 182 nests—the highest total in years—and produced 262 young. That same year biologists in Maine counted 52 active nests and 32 eaglets being raised in that state. Another gain for the Maine eagles was the decision of the Environmental Protection Agency in January, 1979, to deny a water-discharge permit for a proposed oil refinery in Eastport, Maine. The agency ruled that the proposed refinery would threaten the existence of about a dozen pairs of eagles that maintained nests in the area through air pollution, secondary development, and the increased possibility of oil spills.

The Pittston Company, which had planned to build the refinery, promptly appealed the ruling and asked for a review of the situation by the cabinet-level Endangered Species Committee, which had been created specifically to deal with such disagreements. Soon after, the Secretary of the Interior and the company agreed to have the concerned governmental agencies consult once again before submitting the problem to the Endangered Species Committee. Perhaps the expected impact of the refinery on the eagles could be minimized.

On the West Coast, the United States Fish and Wildlife Service acquired 240 acres of private timberland near Klamath, Oregon, in the summer of 1978. Nearly 300 eagles used these acres as a roosting area, and they had been threatened by timbering interests. In Illinois, where bald eagles had not nested for nearly thirty years, public-school students contributed some $55,000 to help purchase eagle wintering refuges along the Mississippi River as part of the state's bicentennial activities. Many other groups and individuals all over the United States were also working in the eagle's behalf. Stanley Wiemeyer, a wildlife biologist in the Environmental Contaminant Program at Patuxent, and his colleagues continued to breed eagles as part of their research. They supplied a number of the eaglets for hacking in New York and Virginia.

"No single organization or governmental action can save a species by itself," declared Lynn A. Greenwalt, Director of the Fish and Wildlife Service, "because it takes a concerted effort and determination of individuals and governmental agencies at all levels to make a lasting impact. But it has been done—with the Key deer, the American alligator, the bison, and with other species. Fortunately for the bald eagle, we have this support, so I am confident it will survive, too."

That confidence was justified, as was clearly shown by the annual census of bald eagles in the forty-eight contiguous states conducted in January, 1979. As reported several months later by the National Wildlife Federation, a total of 9836 bald eagles was counted—nearly twice the number counted in previous surveys. The big total was attributed to the decreased use of harmful pesticides, the many programs being carried on to help the species, and more accurate methods of counting.

3

THE DOWNWARD PLUNGE OF THE BROWN PELICAN

Wings stroking in unison, a dozen brown pelicans skim across the bay in single file, the line of birds rising and falling like the tail of a kite. The widespread gray-and-silver wings beat smoothly for several strokes, then hang suspended for a moment as the birds glide. The pelicans gain altitude and begin to circle. Then, one by one, they dive into a school of fish below them.

From a height of twenty or thirty feet, a brown pelican plummets downward in an almost-vertical corkscrew dive, wings trailing as it plunges into the water. Within a couple of seconds the big bird bobs to the surface, often heading into the wind. If the dive has been successful, the pelican points its bill downward to allow the water to drain out, then upward as it swallows the fish.

brown pelicans in flight

John James Audubon loved to watch the big brown birds as they hunted for food. "The Pelicans follow porpoises pursuing prey, and as the flying fishes rise toward the surface the pelicans come in cunningly for their share of the shoal," he observed. "But a most curious trait of the Pelican is its unwilling service to the Gulls as a sort of purveyor in the way that the porpoises serve Pelicans. The Gull alights on the bill or head of the Pelican and seizes the fish just as the Pelican expels the water from its pouch."

When the bird plunges into the sea to make its catch, the lower jawbones bow outward and the soft-skinned pouch stretches, becoming a very efficient scoop for capturing prey. That remarkable pouch is celebrated in an old familiar limerick:

> A wonderful bird is the pelican.
> His bill will hold more than his belican.
> >He can take in his beak
> >Food enough for a week,
> But I'm damned if I see how the helican.

Written by Dixon Lanier Merritt in 1910, that may be inspired doggerel, but it is certainly inaccurate natural history. The big pouch is used for catching fish, but not for storing them. The prey is swallowed as soon as it is captured.

Life in a Pelican Colony

Exclusive fish eaters, pelicans range along the Atlantic coast from North Carolina southward to Florida, the Gulf states, Mexico, and even as far as the coast of Guyana in South America. They are also found throughout the West Indies. On the Pacific coast they breed from California to northern Chile. Three subspecies are recognized in North America—the eastern, the West Indian, and the western.

Familiar birds in all of these coastal regions and islands, pelicans often follow fishing vessels or gather around wharfs where fishing boats tie up. Dozens of the big brown birds can be seen sitting on wharfs or pilings or paddling in the water as they wait patiently for the boats to dock. Then they scramble for the refuse thrown overboard when the fishermen clean their catch.

As a result of this habit, many pelicans bear fishhooks in their body, or have fishline wrapped about them. Trailing such gear, pelicans often become fatally entangled when they land among mangroves or other trees. One pelican expert estimates that as many as 500 to 1000 die this way every year in Florida.

Pelicans nest in colonies on low offshore islands or sand spits. Their loosely woven nests are constructed of branches, sometimes with an inner lining of leaves or grass. Some may be located on the ground; others are built in low bushes or in the branches of mangrove trees. Both parents take turns incubating the two or three big, chalky, white eggs.

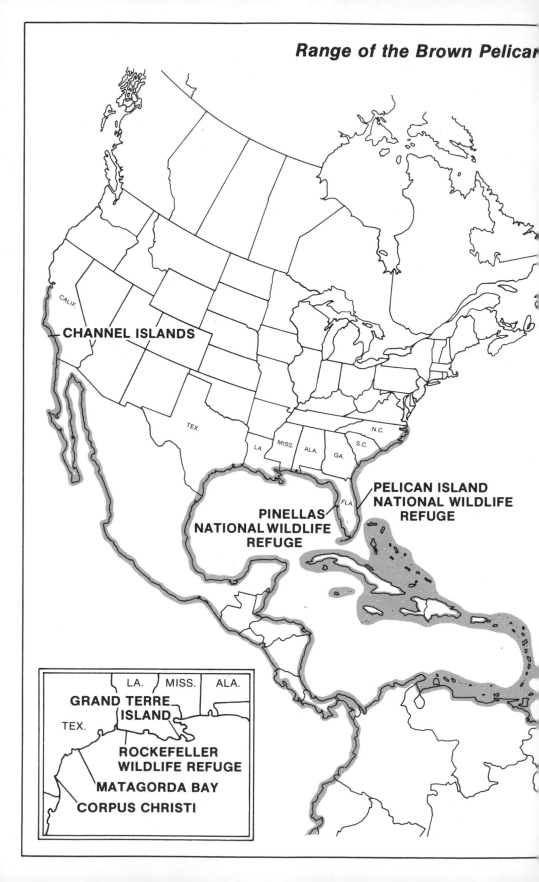

CHANNEL ISLANDS

PELICAN ISLAND
NATIONAL WILDLIFE
REFUGE

PINELLAS
NATIONAL WILDLIFE
REFUGE

CALIF.

TEX.

LA. MISS. ALA. GA. N.C. S.C.

FLA.

GRAND TERRE ISLAND

LA. MISS. ALA.

TEX.

ROCKEFELLER
WILDLIFE REFUGE

MATAGORDA BAY

CORPUS CHRISTI

One of the biggest Florida colonies is on Tarpon Key, a low, doughnut-shaped, mangrove-covered island near the busy Sunshine Skyway that arches over Tampa Bay. Located within thirty miles of a million people or more, Tarpon Key is part of the 377-acre Pinellas National Wildlife Refuge. Ornithologist Ralph Schreiber studied the Tarpon Key pelican colony from 1969 to 1975. In the process, he became one of the country's leading experts on the species. Today he serves as a member of the Eastern Brown Pelican Recovery Team.

During the breeding season, pelicans come and go from the colony all day long. Scores can be seen bathing and preening in the lagoon. Others are in the trees, either incubating eggs, exchanging places after a nest-changing ceremony, or feeding young birds.

A newly hatched pelican chick is a grotesque-looking little creature—naked and wrinkled, with blotched reddish skin and a blunt beak. The chick soon grows a coat of woolly white down. Forever hungry, the youngster eats bits of half-digested fish that the parent bird regurgitates and allows to dribble from the tip of its huge beak. Later on, the young pelican thrusts its head into the open bill of its parent—often deep into the pouch or throat—to snatch pieces of fish.

As they grow up, young pelicans face many hazards. Crows, raccoons, and other predators destroy some eggs and kill some young. Storms and high tides wipe out others. Man's activities also take their toll. Writing more than a century ago, Audubon noted, "If a young bird falls from the nest, it is sure to be seized by some quadruped, or devoured by a shark or barracuda. Indians and others carry them off in quantities. After extensive depredations of this kind the pelicans abandon these breeding places and do not return to them. In fact they are retiring more and more from man's vicinity."

Today land clearing and development have taken away some of the special habitat that pelicans need for successful nesting. The mere presence of people on the breeding grounds has a harmful effect as well. As Audubon noted, when nesting pelicans are disturbed by man they often abandon their eggs or young. Either will die if left exposed to the hot sun too long.

In spite of such hazards, pelicans successfully sustained their numbers over most of their natural range until a quarter of a century ago. They were common and familiar birds to many generations of coastal Southerners and to travelers heading for balmy Southern beaches.

Pelican Colonies in Florida and the Carolinas

One famous Florida colony was located on a tiny three-acre island in the Indian River, just off the east-coast town of Sebastian. Pelican Island, so named because it has long been the locale of a breeding colony, is of historical interest as the first unit in our famed and presently far-flung national wildlife-refuge system.

President Theodore Roosevelt designated Pelican Island a refuge on March 14, 1903, by an executive order proclaiming that the island ". . . is hereby reserved and set apart . . . as a preserve and breeding ground for native birds." The first warden of Pelican Island was Paul Kroegel, appointed and supported by the National Association of Audubon Societies. He remained on the job until 1920, most of this time under Audubon Society supervision.

Today Pelican Island remains a landmark breeding place for pelicans and other aquatic birds, and it is protected and administered by the United States Fish and Wildlife Service. The size of the pelican colony may vary somewhat from year to year. There have been times when a couple of thousand adult pelicans were in residence, with hundreds of nests in the bushes and trees, and young in all stages of development. The 1978 count, however, listed only 100 nests. The island also serves as a breeding ground for cormorants, wood storks, American and snowy egrets, and little blue and Louisiana herons. Man-o'-war birds dip and swoop over the island like giant swallows, and roseate spoonbills sometimes wade through the shallows around the island, probing for food.

All together, there are about ten brown pelican colonies on coastal islands off Florida's east coast, and twice that many on the Florida Gulf coast. There are also a number of small nesting sites on the Florida Keys. As estimated through yearly aerial surveys instituted by Florida's Game and Fresh Water Fish Commission in 1965, the pelican population in the state has remained fairly stable at 6000 to 8000 adult pairs, or 20,000 to 30,000 birds in all. This annual survey is conducted under the direction of Lovett E. Williams, Jr., a veteran wildlife biologist with the commission who has carried out a number of research projects on pelican populations, movements, and nesting success.

Similar aerial surveys in South Carolina in the summer of 1978 revealed a population of approximately 10,000 pelicans there. More than 4000 young birds were fledged in the Palmetto State that same summer—a big increase over previous years. Two of the largest nesting rookeries are those located at Deveaux Bank and at Cape Romain, both north of Charleston. These two rookeries have a combined population of several thousand birds. Most of the

South Carolina pelicans fly south to Florida or the nearby islands for the winter, but between 1000 and 2000 of them spend the cold months in the state where they hatched.

A few hardy pelicans maintain a small northern outpost, breeding on Rock Island, off North Carolina's Outer Bank.

The Pelican Disappears in Louisiana and Texas

Nearly everywhere else in the United States, however, the story has been very different. On the Gulf coasts of Louisiana and Texas, on California's Channel Islands, and other breeding grounds as well, the brown pelican either disappeared completely during the 1960s or was decreasing in numbers so fast that many experts feared it was doomed. By the spring of 1970, pelican populations had been reduced so drastically in these areas that the Fish and Wildlife Service placed both the eastern and western races on its official list of endangered wildlife species.

A half century ago, the brown pelican had been abundant along the Gulf coast, with a total population of 50,000 or more in Louisiana and Texas. Pelicans were still fairly common in both states in the late 1950s, but by 1960 their numbers were shrinking rapidly. During the next several years, almost before anyone realized what was happening, pelicans ceased breeding in these regions and most of the adults disappeared as well.

Louisiana had a special interest in the species' survival, for the pelican is the state bird. The reduction there, however, had evidently started even earlier than it did in Texas, and 1961 marked the last known nesting. A few adult pelicans survived after 1961, but to all intents and purposes the species was extinct in the state.

The Texas pelican population—about 5000 birds in 1920 —had been reduced to about twenty individuals by 1967, with just four nesting attempts that year. In 1968, only two pairs nested. Apparently the brown pelican was just about finished in Texas as well as in Louisiana.

The Role of Pesticides

What caused this spectacular pelican kill in Louisiana and Texas? No one knew for certain, but pesticides were thought to be the probable cause. DDT and other chlorinated hydrocarbons had been used increasingly to control insect pests in Southern croplands during the 1950s and 1960s, and most of these poisons eventually found their way into the Mississippi and other rivers that emptied into the Gulf of Mexico.

In the 1950s, large fish kills were recorded almost every year on the lower Mississippi River; sometimes hundreds of thousands of fish were found floating belly up in the waters. Some investigators believed that pesticides dusted on crops and later draining into streams were responsible. Hard proof, however, was lacking. Fish kills of one kind or another occurred many times each year, so frequently that some people considered them natural.

Then, in November, 1963, an estimated five million fish were killed in the lower Mississippi, and this time biologist Donald Mount of the United States Public Health Service pinpointed the lethal agent. It was endrin, one of the chlorinated hydrocarbons. Through his research, Mount also established the levels of endrin fatal to fish. The poison was manufactured at a chemical plant in Memphis, Tennessee, some 500 miles upriver from New Orleans. Investigation at this plant, in the spring of 1964, showed that endrin wastes were contaminating the waters of the great river. Previous research, such as that conducted after the kill of western grebes at Clear Lake, California, a few years before, had demonstrated the way such poisons—no matter how minute their quantities in the water—become concentrated in ever-increasing densities during each step of the food chain. As fish eaters, pelicans are the last steps in many food chains. Clearly pesticides were a prime factor in their failure to breed.

The late 1950s and early 1960s were also the years when the Department of Agriculture was pursuing most vigorously its fire ant control program in the Southern states. The fire ant, a South American insect that had invaded the United States soon after World War I, had a painful bite. It was a nuisance, but not generally considered a dire threat to crops or people—except by the United States Department of Agriculture. This arm of the Government launched a massive campaign against the fire ant, dumping dieldrin and heptichlor in aerial spraying at the rate of two pounds per acre over most areas. Untold millions of birds, small mammals, fish, and other forms of wildlife perished during the course of the ill-starred campaign. The fire ants, however, were not eliminated.

DDT and its related chlorinated-hydrocarbon pesticides seldom kill large birds such as pelicans outright. Instead, they interfere with the calcium metabolism of the bird, inhibiting the reproductive process and resulting in thin-shelled eggs. Noting this fact, the team that was eventually appointed to oversee the recovery of the eastern brown pelican observed that ". . . there is at this time no adequate explanation for the disappearance of the breeding population (of pelicans) from Louisiana, but the demise of the entire adult population between 1957 and 1961 suggests an extremely lethal agent." From all the evidence, the killing agents had to be pesticides of one kind or another.

In California, the same sort of thing was happening, and

here the pelican reproduction failure was particularly dramatic and well-documented. Thousands of birds had traditionally bred on Anacapa and other Channel Islands off the coast of southern California. In the late 1960s, however, breeding suddenly failed. Dr. Robert Risebrough, a biochemist at the University of California at Berkeley, along with other investigators, uncovered the sad chain of events. From nearly 1000 nesting attempts on Anacapa Island in 1969, only five chicks were known to survive; in 1970, just *one* chick was recorded. Eggs were being broken by the hundreds during incubation, and laboratory tests showed that the pelican eggshells were appreciably thinner than they had been formerly. Analysis of embryos and young showed significant concentrations of chlorinated hydrocarbons in the tissues.

Sunset magazine spread the news in a dramatic poster featuring the brown pelican:

> At most, five young pelicans hatched this year out of 1200 nests in California. All other eggs broke before they hatched, with DDT concentrations of up to 2500 parts per million in the thinnest-shelled eggs.
>
> The pelican eats only marine fish which are now heavily contaminated with both agricultural and industrial pollutants.
>
> No one wants the brown pelican to perish. He does not pollute. He does not slaughter other species. He does not gather together in numbers that nature cannot support.
>
> He is a victim of man—and a warning that man himself may perish, by his own ignorance.

Pursuing his research, Risebrough discovered that the Montrose Chemical Corporation, which had built a plant to manufacture DDT at Torrance, California, in 1947, was emptying huge amounts of chemical residue and wastes into sewers that emptied into the ocean. As many as several thousand pounds of DDT or its equivalent in waste products were being dumped into the coastal waters every day and were affecting sea life for hundreds of miles around.

In October, 1970, the Environmental Defense Fund, a citizen group organized three years before to help protect and monitor the environment, obtained a court injunction to stop Montrose from continuing its dumping practices. Forced to comply, the chemical company sealed the chemical wastes in barrels, which were taken to a nearby landfill site and buried. Faith McNulty, who has chronicled these events in detail in *Audubon* magazine, observes that "What happens when the containers eventually disintegrate will be a problem for future generations."

The pelican die-offs in Louisiana, Texas, and California prompted an even closer monitoring of the fairly stable populations in Florida and the Carolinas. Although there was some fluctuation in numbers from year to year, the annual censuses showed that the Florida and Carolina populations seemed to be holding their own. Laboratory studies of the Florida eggs indicated that their shells were about 10 percent thinner than shells had been in pre-DDT days. Most of the shells, however, were still strong enough to protect the developing young until they hatched. Fortunately, most DDT use had ceased by this time, though the Environmental Protection Agency did not ban it until 1972.

Restoring the Pelican to Louisiana

Louisiana officials were determined to restore their state bird as a breeding species. A definite program to that end started with a meeting in January, 1968, at the Rockefeller

Wildlife Refuge, which was operated by the Louisiana Wildlife and Fisheries Commission at Grand Chenier, on the Mississippi Delta below New Orleans. Attending were representatives from Federal and state wildlife agencies, the National Audubon Society and other conservation organizations, and individuals. One important result of the meeting was the formation of a pelican transplant program, whereby an initial group of fifty fledgling Florida birds were transported to Louisiana that same year. Twenty-six of these fledglings were released on Grand Terre, a low, sandbank island in the Barataria Bay area, to the west of the Mississippi Delta. The others were released at the Rockefeller Refuge in Grand Chenier. All of these latter birds subsequently died, presumably because they were consuming fish that contained high concentrations of DDT and other pesticides brought down by the Mississippi. Thereafter, no more birds were released at Grand Chenier.

From 1969 to 1973, however, yearly releases of young Florida pelicans—some 415 in all—were made in the Barataria Bay area. There the birds flourished. Nesting by three-year-old birds was first reported in the area in 1971, with eight young fledged. Fourteen young were raised in 1972, twenty-six in 1973, and an impressive total of eighty-two in 1974. The pelican was on the way back in Louisiana.

Ted Joanen, Research Leader of the Rockefeller Refuge, was very pleased. "The successful reproduction, eggshell thickness measurements . . . and low DDT body residues in the restocked birds during the period between 1971 and 1974," he noted, "suggests that exceptionally high levels of chlorinated-hydrocarbon pesticides are not present in the pelican's Louisiana environment at this time."

overleaf: brown pelican feeding young

During spring and early summer of 1975, however, disaster suddenly struck this flourishing population of some 465 pelicans in the Barataria Bay area. More than 300 of the birds died—all of them within a short period of time. Autopsies of the dead birds revealed accumulations of seven different pesticides in their tissues, including endrin, dieldrin, toxaphene, and DDE, a metabolic-breakdown product of DDT.

"It's the old food-chain story all over again," declared Allan Ensminger, chief of the Louisiana Wildlife and Fisheries Commission Refuge Division. "What is a very small amount of pesticide in a fish becomes concentrated as it passes up the food chain to the browns. The poison accumulates in the fat of the birds, and in times of stress, such as bad weather or when food is scarce, the pelicans draw on this fat for energy. That's when they die."

DDT had been banned by the Environmental Protection Agency in 1972, but farmers who grew cotton and other crops had turned to the much more potent endrin—which had not yet been banned—as well as to other chlorinated hydrocarbons to combat insect pests. The ban on DDT had been put into effect to safeguard wildlife; but when endrin was used in its place, the results for the pelicans were fatal.

One of the major objectives of the pelican transplant had been to investigate any die-offs very carefully, with the hope that their causes could be pinpointed. The Louisiana pelicans had died so quickly in the summer of 1975, however, that wildlife biologists were unable to accumulate all the evidence they needed to brand endrin as the actual killer, although many of them were sure that it was.

In spite of all the work and dedication of Louisiana's wildlife biologists and those from Florida who had cooperated and advised, the pelican program in Louisiana was in temporary disarray. Still, an additional 100 young Florida pelicans were imported to Louisiana in July, 1975, and released in the Barataria Bay area.

Through 1976, some 765 Florida pelican fledglings were transplanted to Louisiana, and at least 220 young were raised by the restored population of transplanted birds. In the spring of 1977, bad luck struck the restoration project once again when a storm destroyed eighty pelican nests. Afterward, the yearly shipment of 100 Florida pelicans was released in a different location, North Island in the Chandeleur Chain, where the last natural nesting of Louisiana pelicans had occurred in 1961. The pelicans were still having their ups and downs in Louisiana, but they *were* breed-there once again.

The Present Situation in Texas and California

During the early 1970s, the few pelicans in Texas continued to teeter on the edge of oblivion. Almost all of them could be found in the coastal area between Corpus Christi Bay and Matagorda Bay. In these areas, only nine fledglings survived from eleven hatched in 1973, and only two survived from fourteen hatched in 1974. Forty in all were raised from 1964 to 1974.

A transplant program similar to the one in Louisiana was started in 1976. The ultimate success of such undertakings depends, of course, on how well the pesticide ban is enforced, as the Louisiana record clearly shows.

In 1978, a total of thirty-seven young pelicans were fledged at two colonies on Texas offshore islands—an encouraging sign. Another good omen was the sighting on the central Texas coast of more than two hundred young, unbanded birds later that summer. They were thought to be Mexican pelicans that had winged their way north along the Gulf coast to relocate. If such trends continue, Texas may indeed see a restored pelican population in years to come.

In California, too, the situation is much better than it was a few years ago. From just one chick raised on Anacapa Island in 1970, the total increased to thirty-four in 1973, after the release of pesticide wastes into coastal waters was banned. The birds were beginning to recover. A year later some three hundred young were reported on West Anacapa and Santa Cruz Islands. Upward of one thousand nestlings were also counted on Los Coronados Islands, where there had been none in 1969, and just five in 1970. At the same time, the status of the pelican in Mexican waters seemed even more encouraging. Along the west coast of Baja California and in the Gulf of California, there were at least five pelican colonies with populations of 3000 or more pairs each in 1976, and a number of smaller colonies as well.

The good health and survival of brown pelicans, wherever they may be, seem to depend primarily upon an environment reasonably free of the deadly chlorinated-hydrocarbon pesticides. Other important factors include monitoring and safeguarding the condition of coastal waters, so that the bird's fish supply remains abundant, and the protection of breeding colonies from human disturbance.

Brown Pelican Recovery Teams

On September 30, 1975, the Fish and Wildlife Service appointed a recovery team under the leadership of Lovett E. Williams, Jr., to investigate the status of the eastern brown pelican and make recommendations for the bird's recovery to healthy population levels.

"The first goal of the recovery team," the Fish and Wildlife Service reported, "will be to assemble all of the data so far gathered in different parts of the pelicans' range. This will then provide a basis for planning future research and management efforts to accomplish the long-term objective of reestablishing healthy, secure populations of pelicans throughout their former range."

The recovery plan for the eastern brown pelican was issued in February, 1978. It calls for the reestablishment of the Louisiana and Texas populations on all historic nesting sites, the restoration of the pelican to former nesting sites anywhere that are now vacant, and the establishment of new colonies by stocking them with transplants. "The brown pelican became endangered in the first place because of its extreme sensitivity to unknown factors," the team members have concluded. For that reason, all colonies, wherever they are located, need to be closely and continuously monitored. If such a program is carried out, the survival of the brown pelican will be assured.

4

THE CALIFORNIA CONDOR, A DISAPPEARING GIANT

A truck with four-wheel drive stops beside a fire tower overlooking part of Los Padres National Forest, some seventy miles northwest of Los Angeles. Two men get out and unload the carcass of a mule deer killed by a speeding motorist on Highway 99. Placing the carcass in an open meadow some distance from the tower, the men get back in the truck and drive away. That same afternoon other trucks drive to other areas in condor territory and unload the same kind of cargo. The annual condor census—a two-day affair carried out by the California Department of Fish and Game, the United States Fish and Wildlife Service, and other cooperators—is about to begin.

The next morning thirty-six spotters man the fire tower and eleven other observation posts in condor territory.

Seven stations have been baited with deer or goat carcasses. The date is October 13, 1976. The weather is mild, and upward thermals signal good flying weather for the great vultures. At noon the official watch begins. Sometime later one of the observers at the fire tower raises his binoculars and then shouts with excitement. He watches as a speck floats over a distant ridge and gets bigger and bigger. Finally it circles overhead, a huge bird on wings that spread nearly nine feet from tip to tip, with stiff flight feathers extended to either side like probing fingers. Triangles of white on the underside of the wings show that it is an adult condor.

Another condor floats down to join the first one, and then another. By the time the watchers end their vigil at five o'clock that afternoon, sixty different condor sightings have been recorded at this and the other eleven stations. Counting duplications, these sixty sightings probably represent eighteen individual birds. The next day one hundred sightings are recorded. When the data from all stations has been analyzed for probable duplications, and the possibility has been taken into account that some of the surviving condor population has not been counted at all, the census takers come up with an estimate of about forty individual birds.

Those forty birds were most, if not all, of the California condors that survived on Earth in 1976. All of them inhabited a small U-shaped territory bordering the lower end of the San Joaquin Valley in southern California.

A Shrinking Range

The condor's range has not always been so restricted. During the last Ice Age, which ended a mere 10,000 years ago, condors ranged widely over the North American continent. In fact, their fossil remains have been found in Florida. During more recent times, however, the condor was limited to the West Coast region—from Washington and Oregon southward to Baja California. Through the years even that range has steadily shrunk.

One of the first historic records of condors comes from a friar traveling with a band of Spaniards exploring California in 1602. Near Monterey, they sighted a number of the huge birds feeding on a whale carcass. In 1805, more than two centuries later, Lewis and Clark on their epochal exploration of America's Northwestern wilderness sighted condors near the cascades of the Columbia River.

By 1850, the condor had virtually disappeared from Washington and Oregon, and by 1890 most were gone north of San Francisco. By 1900 there were probably no more than an estimated couple of hundred of them left anywhere. What had caused the bird's decline?

Hunters were partly responsible, for they blasted many of the big vultures out of the skies along with eagles, hawks, and other birds of prey. Some condors undoubtedly died from eating poisoned bait put out for wolves, coyotes, and other predators by the farmers and ranchers who were starting to tame California's land. Another factor may have been the likelihood that condors simply were unable to breed successfully when disturbed too much by man. Some ornithologists argued that the condor was a relic from the Ice Age and was doomed to extinction, no matter what.

A Slow Breeder

The individual California condor is a long-lived bird. One yearling bird sent to the National Zoological Park in Washington, D. C., in 1901 survived until 1945. The condor compensates for its long life, however, by being a very

California condor in flight

slow breeder. It does not reach maturity until about eight years of age and may not begin to breed until several years afterward. Then it breeds only every other year, laying just one greenish blue egg each time. That egg is large, measuring close to five inches in length.

Breeding on a secluded, rocky ridge or slope in mountainous country, the birds build no nest as such. The female simply lays her egg on the sandy floor of a shallow cave with a protective overhang, or in a rocky crevice that is sheltered from the weather. In 1950, one pair was discovered nesting in a spacious hole in the trunk of a giant sequoia tree, some ninety-five feet above the ground.

Incubation takes about fifty to sixty days, with both parents sharing the duty. The newly hatched youngster weighs less than a pound and is covered with white down. Its bare head, neck, and feet are pink. After a month, a thick woolly

79

covering of gray down covers the nestling's body including its head. At two months, black pin feathers begin to appear. At three and a half months the youngster may weigh fifteen pounds, but is still no more than half feathered out.

The parent birds look after the young one until it is fully feathered at about six months of age. But it must still learn to fly and soar and hunt for food on its own. The parents continue to feed it until it is a year old or more.

Egg collecting was a popular hobby in the late nineteenth and early twentieth centuries, and collectors vied with one another to secure specimens of the beautiful, rare California condor eggs. In 1895, one commercial dealer offered $250 apiece for three of them. The highest price ever given for a condor egg was perhaps the $300 that a young Californian, Kelly Truesdale, received in 1907. On a backpacking trip into the mountains near San Luis Obispo, he discovered a condor nest on a rocky ledge. Climbing up to the nest, he wrapped the egg he found there in cotton padding, then placed it in a coffee can and lowered it by rope to a companion below.

By this time, the condor was found only in the mountains and foothills of California's Sierra Nevada and the Coast Range surrounding the southern end of the San Joaquin Valley. Perhaps a few others still lived in Baja California, but they all disappeared by the early 1930s.

A Condor Refuge

Very concerned about the condor's dwindling population, the National Audubon Society in 1939 asked Drs. Joseph Grinnell and Alden Miller, of the Museum of Vertebrate Zoology at the University of California at Berkeley, to supervise an extensive study of the species. Just how

80

many condors were there? What were their basic habits and requirements? What were the pressures that were reducing their numbers? What could be done to help them? Carl Koford, a graduate student in ornithology, was selected for the job. He was familiar with the condor country and had been trained in both zoology and forestry.

After observing and studying the big birds from 1939 until 1941, and again in 1946 after he had finished military service, Koford completed his study and wrote a monograph, *The California Condor*, which was published in 1953 by the National Audubon Society. This report was the first detailed and scholarly work ever done on the biology and requirements of the big vulture. In it, Koford emphasized the condor's need for protection from disturbance. In his estimation, no more than fifty or sixty of the big birds remained, and many of their haunts were being invaded by man in increasing numbers.

One of the condor's favorite spots for roosting and bathing was the Sisquoc Falls area in Los Padres National Forest, some eighty miles northwest of Los Angeles. In the mid-1930s, the Forest Service had planned to build a road through this area to make it more accessible to fire fighters, hunters, and fishermen. The project was halted, however, through the efforts of the National Audubon Society and other groups. In 1937, the Forest Service closed 1200 acres around the falls as the Sisquoc Condor Sanctuary.

Some fifty miles east of Sisquoc was the lower Sespe Creek area of Los Padres National Forest, one of the condor's principal breeding grounds. All of this region was open to hunters until 1947, when the Forest Service closed 35,000 acres of it in an effort to protect the condors from disturbance and named it the Sespe Wildlife Preserve. Four years

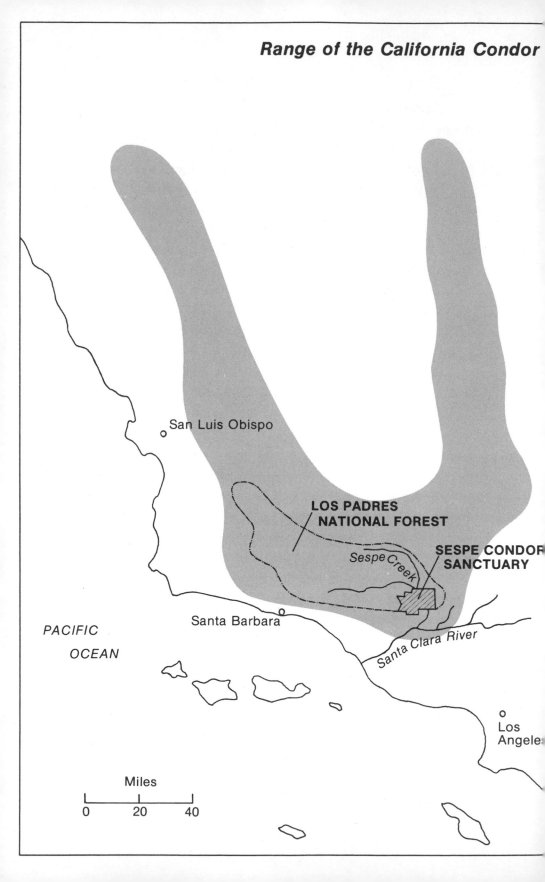

Range of the California Condor

San Luis Obispo

LOS PADRES NATIONAL FOREST

Sespe Creek

SESPE CONDOR SANCTUARY

Santa Barbara

PACIFIC OCEAN

Santa Clara River

Los Angeles

Miles

0   20   40

later the Forest Service enlarged the preserve to 53,000 acres and renamed it the Sespe Wildlife Sanctuary. Later the name was changed to Sespe Condor Sanctuary.

The condors needed all the help anyone could give them. What that help should consist of, however, became a matter of dispute. In 1950, the San Diego Zoological Society was granted a permit by the California Department of Fish and Game to trap several condors in order to attempt breeding the species in captivity. The staff had bred the South American condor successfully in the zoo aviaries and believed that they could do the same with the California condor. They also pointed to the fact that two female condors at the National Zoo in Washington, D. C., had laid more than a dozen eggs between them in the early years of the twentieth century. The experience of the two zoos indicated that California condors could be raised in captivity. San Diego officials thought that the attempt was certainly worth a try.

The San Diego request, however, raised cries of indignation from the National Audubon Society, which at that time believed that all efforts should be put into preserving the birds in the wild, not in raising them in captivity. The controversy was similar to the one raised a few years later over the idea of breeding a captive flock of whooping cranes. In any event, the zoo was unsuccessful in its attempts to trap any wild condors; in 1954, the California legislature rescinded the permit to trap them.

Meanwhile, no one really knew how many condors still survived since Koford's study. Were they increasing, holding their own, or declining? In 1961, the Audubon Society asked for a new study with Alden Miller again supervising the research and the National Geographic Society helping to finance it. The main fieldwork was to be done by Ian and Eben McMillan, two ranching brothers who had lived in the area all of their lives and had turned from egg collectors in their youth to ardent condor conservationists.

The McMillans began their studies in 1963, and the Miller-McMillan report was issued in 1965. Three years later Ian McMillan published a book for the general public, *Man and the California Condor*. The condor population had gone down from an estimated fifty to sixty birds in 1950 to just forty-two in the 1964 count. The prognosis for the species was gloomy.

Threats to the Condor

A number of factors, Miller and the McMillans concluded, were contributing to the decline. Disturbance by hunters and actual shooting of the big birds were still taking their toll, as they had for many years.

Poisoning was always a possibility. The McMillans established that at least six condors had evidently died of poisoning between 1960 and 1964. Ranchers in condor range were accustomed to putting out bait laced with strychnine or other poisons to kill predators. Condors taking the bait would die also. Grain treated with a poison called Compound 1080 (sodium fluoracetate) was frequently scattered in the foothills and in the San Joaquin Valley to kill ground squirrels. If condors ate the squirrels killed in this way, how would they be affected? No one knew for sure.

Pesticides and herbicides were possible threats as well. Again, no one knew just what their effect would be on condor health or reproductive success. DDT and related chlorinated-hydrocarbon pesticides were used in condor territory in the 1950s and 1960s, and later studies showed that some condors carried appreciable amounts of DDT and its derivatives in their body.

A threat of another kind was the 1965 proposal to construct a dam on Sespe Creek, little more than a quarter mile from the nesting sanctuary, and to build a new road to the dam site right through the condor breeding area. The controversy that raged over this proposal was finally laid to rest in 1967, when the voters turned down the proposed dam and road. A victory for the condors.

Finally, oil, gas, and mineral rights were still leased out throughout much of the remaining condor range, and active exploration for these resources was another disturbance for the hard-pressed birds. Not until 1970 did Secretary of the Interior Walter Hickel halt leases for oil and gas in the Sespe area and order a stop to the issuance of any further leases in critical condor areas. Added protection came in 1972–1973, when the United States Forest Service barred firearms from land under its jurisdiction within condor territory, and the California State Legislature prohibited low-flying planes over the Sespe Condor Sanctuary. Court action was needed in 1975 to bar drilling for oil near the Sespe breeding area; in 1976, phosphate mining was also prohibited in some areas adjacent to the condor sanctuaries.

In spite of all these protective steps, the fortunes of the condors seemed to be going from bad to worse. In 1965, when the California Department of Fish and Game started its annual condor census, it tabulated thirty-eight birds. The 1966 census counted a possible fifty-one. Forty-six were seen in 1967, and fifty-three in 1969. In 1971, however, only twenty-eight birds were counted—possibly the result of poor weather conditions. These figures would seem to indicate great fluctuations in the population; actually, they indicate variations in the accuracy of the survey. Any reasonably accurate count depends upon good weather, when condors can be expected to be out hunting for food.

Captive Breeding?

An important development for condors, as well as for other endangered species, occurred when Congress passed the Endangered Species Act of 1966. That same year, Ray Erickson went to Patuxent as Assistant Director for Endangered Wildlife Research. While whooping cranes were one of his main concerns in the early years, he also organized programs for other species. In 1965–1966, nine South American condors were captured in Argentina and brought to Patuxent. A much more numerous species than the California condor, the South American birds could be used to test the possibilities of raising their endangered relatives in captivity and releasing them to the wild.

The only California condor in captivity at that time was a youngster that had been abandoned by its wild parents in 1967. Picked up and taken to the Los Angeles Zoo, it was named Topatopa for the area in which it was found. (Still living at the zoo in the fall of 1978, this condor is scheduled for pairing with another specimen if plans for capturing other wild birds are carried out.)

In 1965, the National Audubon Society appointed its own condor protector and public-relations man in California in the person of John C. Borneman, a dedicated and knowledgeable amateur naturalist and bird man. He roamed condor territory tirelessly and educated the public about condor problems. The condors got another full-time worker in their behalf in 1966, when the United States Fish and Wildlife Service assigned Fred Sibley as its research biologist in charge of condor studies. In 1969, Sibley was succeeded by Sanford R. Wilbur.

Wilbur suggested that one reason condors were not breeding was that they were not getting enough food. In 1971, he instituted a condor-feeding program whereby road-killed deer and other game were placed in the Sespe sanctuary weekly during the breeding season to supplement the supply of carrion. In 1974, this feeding program was expanded and continued on an operational basis the year round.

To bolster the theory that the condors needed more food in order to breed successfully, production of condors in the sanctuary increased somewhat over previous years. Three young condors were raised in Sespe in 1971–1973, where only one young had been raised during the three previous years. Later results have not been so encouraging, however. Condors feed on the carcasses put out for them, but their breeding success has not improved.

Carl Koford believed that supplementary feeding was not necessary. He thought it more likely that pesticides were contributing to condor reproductive failure and proposed research to test that theory, using turkey vultures as the guinea pigs. The Fish and Wildlife Service turned the suggestion down; it had only a limited amount of money available for research, and higher priorities.

Whatever the reasons, the forty or so surviving condors were not reproducing fast enough to maintain even that low number. All observations and research from 1968 on indicated that fewer than two young condors were being fledged each year. "Time is running out," Sanford Wilbur noted pessimistically. Unless the present decline could be stopped, the California condor would inevitably disappear, perhaps as soon as the end of the twentieth century.

Recommendations of the Recovery Team

Sanford Wilbur was designated the team leader of the recovery team appointed by the Fish and Wildlife Service for the California condor. Other members include Borneman and representatives from the California Fish and Game Department, the Forest Service, and the Bureau of Land Management. These governmental organizations control much of the condor range, and their policies and regulations vitally affect the fortunes of the species. By 1973, the team had its Condor Recovery Plan ready—the first such plan completed, as was fitting for the species probably in most danger of imminent extinction. Finally approved in 1975, the plan aimed at maintaining a population of condors that would produce at least four young yearly, more than twice the rate of reproduction at that time. In order to reach this goal, the recovery team proposed an active program that would provide the birds with adequate food as well as roosting and nesting areas. Every effort should be made to reduce condor mortality and educate the public about the bird.

One later, and so far unapproved, proposal is to build artificial nesting sites—simulated rock forms made of fiberglass. These structures could be erected in the vicinity of the Tejon Ranch, a large, privately owned ranch in the Tehachapi Mountains some forty miles northwest of Sespe. There is an abundance of livestock and deer on the Tejon Ranch, and many condors winter there. If they could be induced to nest in the area, chances would be improved for increased numbers of young.

But the recovery team doubted that such efforts would be sufficient to sustain the condors in the wild. As a backup, they proposed a contingency plan that could be put into effect by the fall of 1979 or 1980 if, at that time, the recovery plan was judged ineffective.

This plan proposed the trapping of at least seven condors —three males and four females—over a two-year period.

88

These birds could be teamed up to make four pairs in captivity, if one included the captive Topatopa—thought to be a male—at the Los Angeles Zoo. With a nucleus group of four pairs, a captive-breeding program could be started.

Carl Koford, the original condor expert, took immediate issue with the contingency plan. There were far too few condors in the wild, he declared, to risk upsetting the balance by trying to capture seven birds. There was no proof that they would breed. Even if they did, how could the offspring be introduced into the wild? Koford reiterated his belief that the suspected effects of pesticides on condor reproduction had never been adequately investigated. If they were a contributing factor, the release of captive-bred birds into a polluted landscape would not help the species in the long run. The Fish and Wildlife Service had finally studied condor eggshell fragments from recent years and found deposits of DDT and significant thinning of the shells.

Finally, Koford urged that other experts make an independent evaluation of condor problems before the contingency plan was put into effect. Wilbur agreed and, in December, 1976, asked the American Ornithologist's Union to set up such an advisory panel. It did in 1977, appointing some of the nation's most respected scientists.

Progress at Patuxent

Ray Erickson at Patuxent had his own answers to some of the objections that had been voiced about the contingency plan. He had four active pairs of Andean condors, one pair of which had been breeding at the research station since the spring of 1973, seven years after the first specimens had arrived there—some of them as young birds. By the summer of 1978, nine young had been raised. Erickson had also established that if one egg was taken from a pair, the female would lay another. This discovery was an important one. If a flock of captive breeding condors could be established, the rate of reproduction might be much faster than the normal one of a single chick every two years in the wild.

Several different methods of determining the sex of trapped condors were being investigated. One method, effective only during the breeding season, was to test the sex hormones in the bird's droppings. Another method was the analysis of chromosomes in the feathers. A possible third method was to take a drop of condor blood and measure the weight of DNA in the blood cells. In condors, unlike most other animals, female sex chromosomes weigh less than those of the male. If one or more of these methods could be perfected, the sex of trapped condors could be established.

The Audubon Society, after carefully considering all the alternatives, endorsed the captive-breeding program, convinced at last that lesser activities could not help the condors. Officials at the Los Angeles Zoo began construction of a spacious breeding cage in which Topatopa and a future mate might raise their young.

Recommendations of the Advisory Panel

In the summer of 1978, a year after it had been formed, the condor advisory panel issued its report and recommendations. Although the panel had few criticisms of past condor research and generally subscribed to the recommendations of the Condor Recovery Plan and the contingency plan, it criticized the proposed action program as "short-sighted and unnecessarily conservative."

California condor

In short, the advisory panel recommended expanding the recovery goals to sustaining a population of several hundred wild condors—not just a modest increase over the present population of thirty to forty birds. Indeed, the panel did not believe that there were that many surviving condors; they suspected twenty or thirty birds might be a more accurate count. As for the contingency plan, the advisory panel recommended capturing not just six or seven condors, but a majority of the wild birds. At least ten breeding pairs should be established in captivity, and they should be scattered among several different locations so if anything happened to one group of birds, others would survive elsewhere. Offspring should be kept until adulthood, and there should be at least 100 second- or third-generation birds before any were released. Then, only second- or third-generation birds should be considered for release. The advisory panel recommended a release method similar to hacking, as had been used to reintroduce peregrine falcons, eagles, and other birds of prey to the wild.

The panel was suggesting a program that would take thirty or forty years to complete, with no guarantee that it would succeed until it had been tried. And, as Keith Schreiner, Associate Director of the Fish and Wildlife Service noted, it could well take twenty-five to thirty million dollars to carry it out. Would the public back such an outlay?

Even the most optimistic proponents of captive breeding concede that it will take at least a human generation—perhaps more—to assess success or failure. Still, if the plan is not attempted, the species seems to be doomed to extinction by the end of this century, or soon thereafter.

As the year 1978 drew to a close, the Fish and Wildlife Service was still undetermined whether to start such a program of captive breeding of California condors. Meanwhile, census takers observed only an estimated twelve or thirteen birds in October of that year. This count was not a total one, however, for at least that many birds had been recorded in a single flock the month before. After going through all the data, Sanford Wilbur noted, ". . . it looks like the population actually includes about thirty birds, a continuing and rather drastic decline in only a few years." One wild chick had been raised in 1977, but Wilbur had been unable to confirm any nesting in 1978. He added, ". . . . hopefully, there was some, but I don't think we can expect more than one young bird this year."

Little by little, time seems to be running out for the California condor.

5

THE
MYSTERY
OF
THE
KIRTLAND'S
WARBLER

In the second week of October, 1841, Samuel Cabot, Jr., of Boston, was bound for Yucatán, where he looked forward to studying and collecting the birds of this little-known area. As his ship was sailing between the Bahaman island of Abaco and Cuba, a little warbler dropped down on the ship to rest, and Cabot collected it as a specimen. After preparing it as a skin, he packed it away and paid little further attention to it. As a later ornithologist was to note, he was evidently "so preoccupied with his studies of the spectacular tropical birds of a country entirely untouched by ornithologists that the little Bahama warbler skin, brought back to Boston and deposited in his collection, remained unnoticed." Not until twenty-one years later was his prize—the first specimen of record ever taken of Kirtland's warbler—

identified as such. By then, however, other specimens had been collected and the bird was recognized as a new species.

The type specimen of Kirtland's warbler—the one used for the scientific description of a new species—was collected on May 13, 1851, nearly ten years after Cabot's journey. It was shot on the Ohio farm of Dr. Jared P. Kirtland, a noted doctor and naturalist, by his son-in-law, Charles Pease. This type specimen was a male bird in breeding plumage—gray strongly flecked with black above, a black facial mask, and lemon-yellow breast.

Pease turned the specimen over to Dr. Kirtland, an expert on the birds of Ohio. The doctor quickly realized that the bird represented a species he had never seen before and passed it on to his good friend and fellow ornithologist, Spencer Baird, the Assistant Secretary of the Smithsonian Institution in Washington. Baird officially described the new species the next year and named it in honor of Dr. Kirtland. Neither he nor anyone else knew anything about the habits and life history of the bird.

In the course of the next twenty-seven years, five more specimens were collected during spring migration: four in Ohio and one in Michigan. Where had they wintered? Where did they nest? No one knew the answers. The wintering grounds were finally discovered on January 9, 1879, when Charles B. Cory collected a Kirtland's warbler on Andros Island in the Bahamas, not far from the place where Samuel Cabot had collected his shipboard specimen nearly thirty-eight years before.

Discovery of the Breeding Grounds

The bird's breeding grounds remained a mystery until the twentieth century. In June, 1903, E. N. Frothingham, an ornithologist with the Museum of Zoology at the Uni-

versity of Michigan, went on a fishing trip with his friend
T. G. Gale along the Au Sable River in Michigan's Lower
Peninsula. While there, they heard an unfamiliar birdsong—
a short one-and-a-half-second outpouring that was repeated
again and again in rapid succession, sometimes as often as
ten times in a minute. Finally they located the singer, and
Gale shot it. Frothingham took the specimen back to the
museum and showed it to Norman Wood, the Curator of
Ornithology. Wood identified it as a Kirtland's warbler
and realized that it must have been on its breeding grounds.
He promptly set off for the area where the bird had been
collected and began to search for other specimens, and especially for a nest. For eight frustrating days he searched
in vain. He heard the male's song over and over, and he
sighted individual birds. Finally, he began to search
through an area that had been swept by fire several years
before, in which young jack pines were growing thick and
lush. His field notes describe the event:

> I have just found a pair of Kirtland's warblers and,
> as I write, the female is three feet away, fluttering her
> wings. . . . The male is on top of a dead stub twenty
> feet high. . . . I saw him go down and went over
> there. . . . Down into the jack pine he went. . . .
> No bird and no nest! . . . I began looking carefully
> on the ground, as I had made up my mind that it
> would be found there. Suddenly I saw the nest! In [it]
> were two young birds a few days old, and, as luck
> would have it, one beautiful egg . . . pinkish white,
> thinly sprinkled with chocolate brown spots gathered
> in a wreath at the larger end.

The nest of a Kirtland's warbler is almost invisible—

a snug pocket of grasses and fine plant material built on the ground or close to it, concealed beneath the shelter of the low, sweeping branches of young jack pines. About the only way a person can find it is to locate the singing male and watch where the bird drops to the ground. During the breeding season, a male warbler may sing his short song as many as 2000 times between sunup and sundown, a sure signal for those who recognize it.

Early Field Studies

For twenty years or more after the discovery of the rare warbler's breeding place, little serious research was done on the species. The evident limits of its range were staked out, however: parts of twelve counties in Michigan's Lower Peninsula, an area of about one hundred by sixty miles. To this day, no nest has ever been found further than sixty miles from the place where Wood found the first one. All of the nesting colonies are located in areas of burned-over jack pine.

When prolonged research on the species finally did begin, Wood's students led the way. In 1922, a promising undergraduate, Nathan Leopold, became interested in Kirtland's warbler and began to study it. That summer he and a friend searched the area where Wood had found the original nest, but had no luck. Leopold correctly surmised that perhaps the area had changed so much in twenty years that it no longer afforded suitable breeding places for the bird. The young jack pines had perhaps grown too tall and no longer had the sweeping lower branches that helped to hide the nests so effectively.

Persisting, Leopold returned to the same general region the next year, and in a different area finally heard the

97

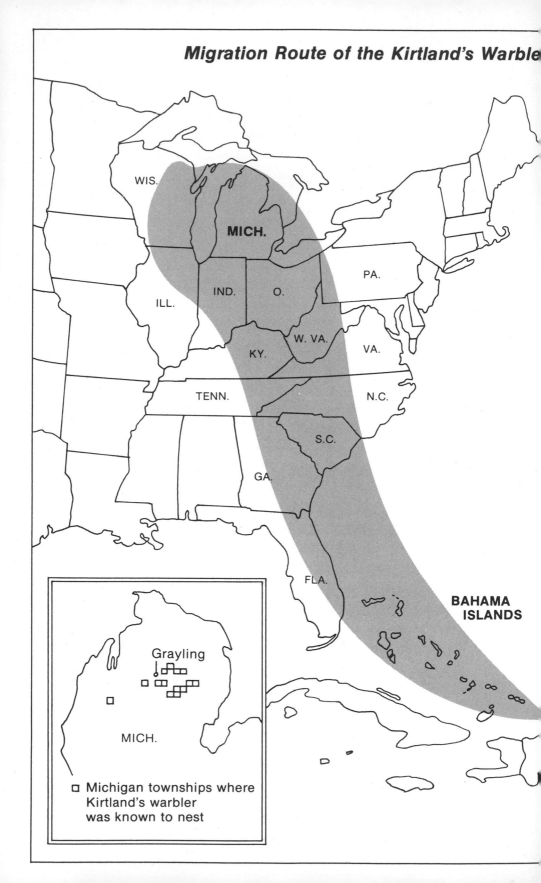

Migration Route of the Kirtland's Warbler

WIS.

MICH.

PA.

IND.

O.

ILL.

W. VA.

KY.

VA.

TENN.

N.C.

S.C.

GA.

FLA.

BAHAMA ISLANDS

Grayling

MICH.

☐ Michigan townships where Kirtland's warbler was known to nest

breeding song and located several nests. One had a single baby warbler in it, and also a much larger nestling of a brown-headed cowbird.

Cowbirds are parasitic birds, laying their eggs in the nests of other species and leaving them for the foster parents to raise. Often they remove one or more of the rightful eggs as well. The usual warbler clutch is four or five eggs, and the incubating period averages fourteen days, whereas that of the cowbird is two days shorter.

Leopold was the first person to recognize that cowbirds were a potential threat to the rarer and smaller bird. He noted the danger in an account he wrote for the January, 1924, issue of *The Auk*, the official publication of the American Ornithologists' Union:

> It has long been a subject of speculation why the Kirtland's warbler, which raises as large a brood as most other warblers, and which apparently has no more natural enemies than the other warblers, should continue to be so extremely scarce. I suggest as a reason for this fact that the bird is largely preyed upon by the cowbird. Whenever we saw a singing male Kirtland's there were a number of cowbirds perched about in the tall dead trees, apparently in quest of the same thing for which we were looking. . . . it is greatly to be feared that *D. kirtlandii* may soon be another of the American birds on the extinct list.

The Continuing Research of Van Tyne and Mayfield

The next person who devoted a great deal of time to research on the species was one of Wood's graduate stu-

overleaf: Kirtland's warbler feeding chicks

dents, Jocelyn Van Tyne, who would eventually succeed him as Curator of Birds at the University of Michigan Museum of Zoology. Van Tyne began his doctorate in 1925, and over the years collected reams of material about the warbler. He said that his book on the species would be his life's work, but when he died in 1957 no manuscript was found, only innumerable notes written on three-by-five cards. It remained to Harold Mayfield, a highly skilled amateur ornithologist who made his living as the personnel director for a large manufacturing company, to write finally the definitive work on the species. His book, *The Kirtland's Warbler*, was published by the Cranbrook Institute of Science in 1960.

Mayfield was a longtime friend of Van Tyne, and from 1944 until Van Tyne's death in 1957 had accompanied him on his annual field trips to the warbler's breeding grounds. Van Tyne recognized that the cowbird was a threat to the warbler, but he never considered it the primary enemy. In his opinion, the main requirements for the warbler were sufficient suitable breeding and wintering habitat.

After Van Tyne's death, Mayfield continued the research on his own. There were a number of fascinating but puzzling aspects to the case of the Kirtland's warbler.

In the first place, the nesting requirements of the species are very specialized. The Kirtland's warbler will nest only under young jack pines that are between six and twenty feet tall. Before they are five or six years old, the jack pines are hardly large enough to shelter and conceal the nests. After fifteen years, they are too mature. The lower limbs of the trees have died by this time, and the low shelter the bird seems to need is not present. Because of this specialized breeding requirement, the Kirtland's warbler is often

102

known by the alternate common name of jack-pine warbler.

Furthermore, the extreme heat of a forest fire is needed to open the jack-pine cones so the seeds can pop out. Only after flames have swept through an area of mature jack pines will seeds drop to the ground, take root, and begin to reforest the region.

All Kirtland's warbler nests except one have also been found in a distinctive sandy soil, called "Grayling soil" for the town around which it is most prevalent. Grayling soil is highly porous and affords good drainage, a very important factor for nests built on the ground.

In 1957, the Michigan Department of Natural Resources set aside three different tracts of four square miles each—about 7700 acres in all—as warbler management areas. The United States Forest Service followed suit in 1961 by setting aside a warbler management area of more than 4000 acres in Huron National Forest. Each of these large areas is subdivided into a number of smaller ones. In rotation, every five years, one of these smaller areas is burned off in a controlled fire (Operation Popcone) in order to provide suitable conditions for young jack pines to sprout. The overall burning cycle for all areas is fifty to sixty years. Before each controlled burn, all except a few seed trees are cut in the area. In this way suitable breeding habitat for the warbler can be provided on a continuing basis.

In 1951, Mayfield organized a census of the Kirtland's warbler. A group of thirty-two census takers ranged through the breeding territory and counted 432 singing males, indicating a population of 864 breeding adults. A similar census was taken in 1961, ten years later, and showed 502 singing males—an encouraging increase that pointed to a total population of over 1000 birds. But the 1971 census was very discouraging: only 201 singing males, or about 40 percent of what the population had been ten years before. What was the matter?

Mayfield noted that the range of the warbler had diminished as well, and it seemed to be shrinking in toward the center of the former twelve-county range. Today the species is found in only eight sizeable breeding colonies located in three counties.

Victimized by the Cowbird

Throughout his years of observation and research, Mayfield came more and more to realize what a serious problem the cowbirds posed to Kirtland's warbler. He had seen how parasitized nests produced far fewer young warblers than those that were not parasitized.

Brown-headed cowbirds are nomadic birds that originally followed the great buffalo herds in their yearly travels over the short-grass prairies of the West. Not accustomed to staying in one place long enough to build nests and raise their own young, the females searched out the nests of many other birds—over 150 species are recorded as being victimized—and deposited their eggs in them. When the buffalo herds vanished, the cowbirds adapted to changing circumstances. They began to follow cattle and pushed into Eastern farm country, continuing to lay eggs in other birds' nests.

Different species of birds cope with this problem in different ways. Some abandon their nests when they find cowbird eggs in them and start over in a new location. Some wall off the offending cowbird eggs or build a new nest floor over them, and then they lay a new clutch of their own. Others simply incubate the cowbird eggs as well as their own and care for the young cowbirds when they hatch. That is what the Kirtland's warbler does, usually with disastrous results for its own young. For one thing, baby cowbirds have the vital advantage of a two-day start over the newly hatched warblers. The cowbird is much larger to begin with, and by the time it is two days old it weighs eight times as much as the newly hatched warbler. As a result, the cowbird nestling takes a greater share of the food, and it often tramples the smaller warbler babies to death or shoves them out of the nest.

Mayfield observed the cowbird-warbler relationship with growing disquiet. His research over the years indicated that for every one hundred warbler eggs in nests parasitized by cowbirds, only twenty-two on the average survive to the fledgling stage. Forty-one of those one hundred warbler eggs are removed from the nest by adult cowbirds. Six fail to hatch because they get shoved aside or because the cowbird eggs hinder their incubation. Just fifty-three warbler nestlings hatch from the one hundred eggs, and thirty-one of them die because they cannot compete with the bigger and stronger cowbird young.

When the 1971 census showed just 201 breeding pairs of Kirtland's warblers, Mayfield and other experts decided that drastic steps needed to be taken. A limited program of cowbird control was begun in 1971, and the next year it was expanded in an all-out attempt to get rid of cowbirds in the warbler nests by trapping them. This program was a cooperative effort with the Michigan Audubon Society providing the materials for the traps, the Michigan Department of Natural Resources constructing them, and the Fish and Wildlife Service and the Forest Service tending the traps and disposing of the captured birds.

105

The traps themselves were large box structures, measuring about sixteen feet long and six feet wide and high, and covered with chicken wire. The entrance was on the top of the cage, a wide funnel covered with a large-gauge mesh that allowed the birds to find their way in but not out. The cages were baited with sunflower seeds.

Fifteen such traps were used in 1971, and about 2000 cowbirds were taken. After that first year, up to thirty-eight traps were used, and from 3100 to 4300 cowbirds were trapped each season. In six years a total of 17,529 cowbirds were removed.

During the early stages of the program, captured cowbirds were taken many miles away and released. When it was discovered that those same birds soon returned to the area, the captives were quickly and painlessly gassed to death. Some animal lovers disapprove of such tactics. Most conservationists and wildlife biologists, however, believe that it is justifiable and necessary to destroy individuals of a common species in certain areas or under particular circumstances, when those common species pose a distinct threat to an endangered species.

Other kinds of birds caught in the traps were either freed on the spot or removed to distant areas and then released. This treatment was given to blue jays, which will eat warbler eggs if they find them.

An Uncertain Future

After two years of such aggressive control, the 1973 census showed 216 singing male warblers, a slight but encouraging improvement over the 1971 census of 201 singing males. In 1974, however, the count dropped to just 167 males. This decrease indicated a rapidly shrinking population of little more than 300 birds. All of the efforts being

singing male Kirtland's warbler

expended in behalf of the Kirtland's warbler seemed to be in vain.

Some ornithologists believed that the low total was due to high overwintering losses, especially of young birds. From banding records and other observations, the survival rate for the first year seemed to be only about 20 percent— evidently only one of five fledglings lived to return to Michigan's Lower Peninsula the next spring. Were these first-year losses due to a high death rate for the fledgling birds during their first summer? Did the attrition come during the long migration flights to the Bahamas and back? Or were the losses occurring on the wintering areas?

Research and direct observation in Michigan had demonstrated that cowbird control was giving the individual Kirtland's warbler more chance of survival than ever. The 1977 census indicated a good nesting year, with a total of 218 singing males or 436 adult birds; 131 eggs had been laid, and 66 young fledged. The 1978 census, however, counted only 193 singing males, a more than 10 percent decrease in less than a year. Even so, individual nesting had been excellent. "This year, Mr. Walkinshaw [a retired dentist who was also a skilled ornithologist and Kirtland's-warbler expert] found three nests, each with six eggs," declared John Byelich of the Michigan Department of Natural Resources and leader of the Kirtland's Warbler Recovery Team. "Only once in the last thirty years has he found a nest with so many eggs. We attribute this to cowbird removal."

The program of cowbird removal continues, and the warblers are being monitored even more closely than before, but the species is still not responding as ornithologists believe it should. Trying a new tack in February, 1978, they instituted a search in Wisconsin for typical Kirtland's warbler breeding grounds of young jack pines in burned-over areas of Grayling soil. When the breeding season arrived, tapes of male birds singing were played in likely spots to try to determine whether any Kirtland's warblers were in residence. Two singing males were discovered, but no evidence of nesting activities.

Warbler counters in Michigan also expanded their search and spotted four unmated males in widely scattered sections of the Lower Peninsula. In addition, one lone male was discovered singing in the Province of Ontario in Canada and still another one turned up in Quebec. The possibility had to be considered that Kirtland's warbler might breed in some sites that had never been spotted by observers.

The fate of Kirtland's warbler is still uncertain, and the mystery that surrounds its fluctuating fortunes continues. What are the actual factors that limit the population? Today researchers are doing their best to find the answers to that question.

The Kirtland's Warbler Recovery Team has set a goal of 1000 pairs of breeding Kirtland's warblers. To support that many birds, about 135,000 acres of warbler management area will be needed. If the population should drop to even more dangerous levels than at present, the recovery team believes that plans should be made to start a transplant program. This procedure would be especially useful if the species does not respond more positively to current management efforts.

In a transplant program, eggs of nesting Kirtland's warblers would be substituted for the eggs of other local, unendangered species. Like many other birds, the female Kirtland's warbler usually lays another clutch of eggs if her first clutch is removed. Thus, the number of fledgling warblers might be doubled every year as a result of a successful transplant program.

6

SEARCH
FOR
THE
IVORY-BILLED
WOODPECKER

The flash of a bright-red crest, a streak of gleaming white against glossy black feathers—a big woodpecker flies swiftly through the Southern lowland forest on wings that spread thirty inches from tip to tip. On the bird goes, past giant oaks and maples, over tangled stands of gum and bay trees. It is a male ivory-billed woodpecker in flight.

Swooping down, the big woodpecker lands on its nest tree, a giant sweet gum. Propped against the trunk by its stiff, tapered tail, it trumpets its call—a loud, staccato *kent, kent, kent!* The bird's long stout bill is ivory white; the black of its body feathers is accented by the broad white stripe running from each cheek down the neck and merging into a large white wing patch.

Climbing up the trunk, the male bird is greeted at the

110

nest hole by his mate. She is identical in her markings, except that her crest is black, not red. The female flies off to hunt for food, and the male enters the nest hole to take his turn incubating the three white eggs at the bottom of the cavity.

The pileated woodpecker, a slightly smaller and always more plentiful woodpecker, is sometimes confused with its larger relative, the ivorybill. The pileated, however, shows no white on its back when it is resting; in flight it displays white on the forward instead of the trailing portion of its wings, and both sexes have red crests. The calls of the two species are quite different, too. The ivorybill utters loud, trumpetlike toots, while the call of the pileated is rather like that of a flicker. One ornithologist likens it to the cry of a frightened chicken.

The ivory-billed woodpecker hunts for its food in a very distinctive manner, leaving unmistakable evidence of its having been feeding in an area. Its chief food consists of large grubs of wood-boring beetles that live between the bark and sapwood of recently dead hardwood trees. Attacking the tightly fastened bark with powerful swipes of its stout bill, the big woodpecker sends splinters flying in all directions. Sometimes it removes practically all of the bark over a considerable portion of the trunk or a large limb. The smaller pileated woodpecker usually searches for its food in trees that have been dead for some time and probes deeply into the decaying wood without stripping off so much bark. It makes distinctive rectangular nest openings in a tree, while the nest hole of the ivorybill is oval.

Prized for Its Plumage and Bill

In Colonial days, the ivorybill ranged through lowland and coastal areas from eastern North Carolina to Louisiana

111

and eastern Texas, and up the valley of the Mississippi and its principal tributaries to Oklahoma, Missouri, southern Illinois, and Indiana. It lived where there were extensive mature stands of hardwood trees such as oak, sweet gum, maple, and cypress. The nest was usually excavated forty to sixty feet up in a tree, and the cavity itself was from twenty to twenty-four inches deep.

The ivorybill has long been an uncommon bird in most areas. The early English naturalist Mark Catesby traveled extensively in America between 1712 and 1725, and he considered it rare then. More than a century afterward, however, Audubon noted that it was "very abundant along the Buffalo Bayou near Houston, Texas." He did not find it in such numbers anywhere else, however.

The species was prized by hunters, who wanted the bird for its decorative plumage and distinctive bill. "Travellers of all nations are also fond of possessing the upper part of the head and the bill of the male," Audubon observed, "and I have frequently remarked, that on a steam-boat's reaching what we call a *wooding-place*, the *strangers* were very apt to pay a quarter of a dollar for two or three heads of this Woodpecker. I have seen entire belts of Indian chiefs closely ornamented with the tufts and bills of this species, and have observed that a great value is frequently put upon them."

Audubon himself took his share of the big and beautiful birds, and he ridiculed those who questioned the prices

ivory-billed woodpecker

113

asked for their skins. "I have heard the amateur or closet-naturalist express his astonishment that half-a-crown was asked by the person who had perhaps followed the bird when alive over miles of swamps, and after procuring it, had prepared its skin in the best manner, and carried it to a market thousands of miles distant from the spot where he had obtained it."

Alexander Wilson Captures an Ivorybill

Alexander Wilson, Audubon's slightly older contemporary and also an enthusiastic student of American birds, tells an amusing story about his experiences with an ivory-billed woodpecker. Sighting the bird in a tree near Wilmington, North Carolina, Wilson promptly shot at it. It fell to the ground with a minor wing injury. Rushing forward, Wilson threw his coat over the bird and wrapped it up. He wanted the living bird to paint and may also have thought he could tame it, as he had once tamed a Carolina parakeet.

"I carried it with me in the chair, under cover, to Wilmington," he related. "In passing through the street, its affecting cries surprised everyone within hearing, particularly the females, who hurried to the doors and windows with looks of alarm and anxiety." The bird's cries, to his discomfort, sounded remarkably like those of a heartbroken child.

Arriving back at his hotel, Wilson left the injured bird in his room while he went out to look after his horse. Returning a short time later, he found his bed covered with plaster from an opening some fifteen inches wide in the ceiling. There was a second, somewhat smaller hole near a window. The prisoner had not been idle!

To prevent it from doing any more damage, Wilson

114

knotted a piece of string around the woodpecker's leg and tied it to the foot of a mahogany table. He then left the room a second time. When he returned he found the table riddled by the sledgehammer blows of the bird's beak. Despairing of either taming or controlling his captive, Wilson decided to paint it as quickly as possible. "While engaged in taking the drawing," Wilson admitted, "he cut me severely in several places, and, on the whole, displayed such a noble and unconquerable spirit, that I was frequently tempted to restore him to his native woods. He lived with me nearly three days, but refused all sustenance, and I witnessed his death with regret."

A sad ending for a spirited captive. Unfortunately, Wilson neglected to record what the hotel owner thought about the whole episode.

Hunters such as Wilson, Audubon, and others helped to reduce the ivorybill's numbers. In just two years in the late nineteenth century, one professional collector, A. T. Wayne, received seventeen specimens of the birds from hunters in the Suwanee River region of Florida. Another bagged twenty-nine specimens in a three-year period, and forty in all during his lifetime, when the species was already quite rare.

Research on the Species in the Singer Tract

The loss of suitable habitat, however, was what really spelled the downfall of the species. The years between 1885 and 1910 were the heyday of the lumbering industry in the South, the period when great stands of cypress and other hardwoods were being cut. They were also the time when the ivorybill was disappearing nearly everywhere.

By 1915, the ivory-billed woodpecker seemed to be confined to perhaps a dozen scattered areas in South Carolina,

Florida, and Louisiana, where remnants of the once-endless cypress swamps and Southern hardwood forests still survived. By 1925, however, a number of these regions had also been cut over. Some ornithologists considered the ivorybill already extinct; if not extinct, it was certainly on the brink of that ultimate fate.

Yet a few of the birds still survived in certain areas. In 1935, Dr. Arthur A. Allen, the well-known Cornell ornithologist and teacher, studied several pairs of breeding birds in the Singer Tract, an 80,000-acre tract of hardwood forest in north-central Louisiana named for its owner, the Singer Sewing Machine Company. Allen took photographs of the birds and recorded their calls. One of his graduate students in ornithology, James T. Tanner, accompanied him.

Stirred to action by the imminent possibility of the woodpecker's disappearing, the National Audubon Society backed Tanner in a study of the species, with the hope that some way might be found to help it. Although he searched for the bird in many areas of possible habitat, Tanner did most of his work in the Singer Tract. He continued his studies there until 1939, when he received his advanced degree at Cornell on the basis of his research. His book, *The Ivory-billed Woodpecker*, published in 1942 by the National Audubon Society, is still considered the definitive work on the species.

Tanner confirmed the specialized feeding habits of the ivorybill and came to the reluctant conclusion that it was doomed if the big stands of hardwood forests continued to disappear. One pair of ivorybills, he noted, needed at least six square miles of forest in order to find enough mature trees that were dead or dying. Only in such trees could the birds find the beetle grubs they needed. The pileated

116

woodpecker did not require such large areas because its food was not so specialized.

Tanner estimated that about twenty-two ivorybills lived in the Singer Tract at the time of his studies. He thought that some individuals also survived in the Santee River valley of South Carolina and in three different areas of Florida. During World War II the Singer Tract was cut over for its lumber, and the last ivorybill recorded there was spotted in 1944. The species seemed close to extinction. But, time after time, people continued to come forward claiming that they had seen or heard the birds in one place or another.

Okefenokee Swamp in southern Georgia—a vast swamp with large stands of mature cypress trees— would seem to be a good area for the bird, and indeed one was recorded as having been shot there in 1941. Then a pair of the big woodpeckers was reported as having been seen in the swamp in 1948. Afterward nothing.

Two years later Whitney Eastman, a naturalist from Minneapolis, claimed that he had seen a male ivory-billed woodpecker in the Chipola River Swamp in Florida on March 3, 1950. The next day, he reported, he saw a female as well. In April of the next year, John V. Dennis, a well-known woodpecker expert from Virginia, said that he had heard the distinctive call of an ivory-billed woodpecker in the same area. He did not see the bird, however.

Nearly ten years later, Clarence Cottam, a highly respected ornithologist and wildlife expert, reported in 1961 that two pairs of ivorybills and a single bird had been sighted somewhere in eastern Texas. He would not say just where. He feared that enthusiastic birders and collectors, if they knew the location, would inevitably congregate there and either chase the birds away or kill them. Another specimen was reportedly seen in North Carolina that same year.

Such reports and rumors of ivorybills continued. By 1966, however, nearly a quarter of a century had passed since the last verified sighting. Financed by a grant from the World Wildlife Fund that year, John Dennis headed for the Big Thicket country in the Neches River valley of eastern Texas to check out persistent rumors of the bird. A vast expanse of swamps, tea-colored streams, impenetrable thickets, and extensive stands of hardwood trees, the Big Thicket had once covered more than three million acres, but by this time had been reduced to about one tenth that size.

The next year, Dennis declared he had hit the jackpot. Exploring the Big Thicket on December 3, 1966, he heard an ivorybill; on the tenth, a week later, he saw one. During a later trip, financed this time by the Department of the Interior, he reported that he had seen another specimen on February 19, 1967. All together, he figured, the Big Thicket country supported perhaps five to ten pairs of ivorybills. He had made a three-minute recording of the bird's calls, but the quality of the record was marred by extensive background noise, and its authenticity has been a subject of dispute ever since. Neither Dennis nor anyone else had come up with convincing *proof* of the ivorybill's survival in Texas or anywhere else. As a result of Dennis's claims, however, Secretary of the Interior Stewart Udall announced that the Bureau of Sport Fisheries and Wildlife would investigate other purported recent sightings of ivorybills in several other areas: along the Congaree River in South Carolina; along the Apalachicola River in Florida; in the valley of the Tombigbee River in Alabama and Mississippi; and around the Altamaha River in Georgia. This

118

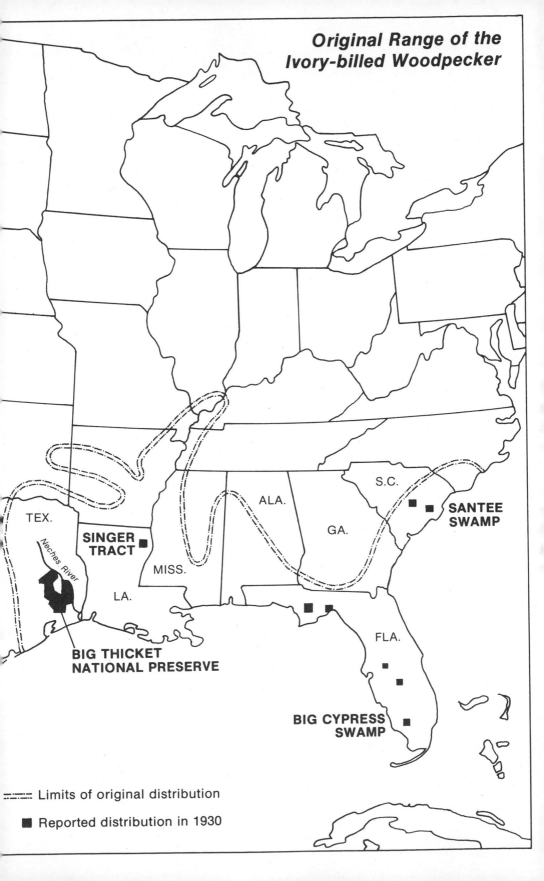

Original Range of the Ivory-billed Woodpecker

S.C.

ALA.

GA.

TEX.

SINGER TRACT

MISS.

LA.

Neches River

SANTEE SWAMP

BIG THICKET NATIONAL PRESERVE

FLA.

BIG CYPRESS SWAMP

Limits of original distribution

Reported distribution in 1930

project was carried out, but with no positive results. Dennis, joined by James Tanner and Paul W. Sykes, Jr., a Federal biologist, subsequently searched the Neches River area in Texas once more. No certain sightings resulted, and both Tanner and Sykes were skeptical about their being any ivorybills in the Big Thicket.

Dennis's reports did, however, spark one very positive action. In considerable measure due to the publicity surrounding his Big Thicket claims, Congress set aside funds for purchase of land, and the Big Thicket National Preserve—twelve separate woodland units and connecting river corridors, about 85,000 acres in all—was signed into law in 1974.

Does the Ivorybill Survive Anywhere?

The question persisted, however: Did ivory-billed woodpeckers survive anywhere? And if any did, would their fresh carcasses be needed to prove that they had recently been among the living?

John Dennis had a theory that explained the elusive quality of the species: the ivorybill is—and was—a "disaster species" and a nomad. It lived in areas where fires and hurricanes had killed many mature hardwood trees and where it could find plenty of beetle grubs in the recently dead trees. When the food was used up, it moved to some other area. It would do the same when its habitat was disturbed or cut over. This reasoning explained why the species could be reported in one place, later disappear, then be reported in another area. Many other ornithologists, however, were unconvinced that the ivorybill moved about in this fashion.

In Florida, two amateur naturalists claimed that over an extended period, from 1967 through 1969, they had located the species in a swamp in the central part of the state and had either seen or heard the birds on eleven different occasions. They had also discovered nesting holes. One of the nesting trees had fallen, and in it the two bird watchers found several feathers, which were forwarded to the dean of American ornithologists, Dr. Alexander Wetmore of the Smithsonian Institution. He identified one of them as indeed the feather of an ivorybill. "It could have been twenty years old," he added.

On March 14, 1971, another report came in. Robert Manns, a Southern representative of the Audubon Society, played an ivorybill tape recording—the same one that Arthur Allen had recorded in the Singer Tract many years before—in South Carolina's Santee Swamp. Much to his amazement, he reported, the distinctive call of an ivorybill was heard in response. But he did not see the bird.

Six months later came one of the most controversial reports of all. In the National Audubon Society's publication *American Birds,* for October, 1971, was a report: "On May 22, 1971, a pair of ivory-billed woodpeckers was seen and photographed 'somewhere in Louisiana.'" The item had been sent in by Dr. George H. Lowery, Jr., one of America's most respected ornithologists, founder and director of the Museum of Natural Science at Louisiana State University. The observer, an avid bird watcher, had shown the pictures to Dr. Lowery. After careful checking, he agreed that they were indeed photographs of ivorybills. The pictures had been taken with a cheap camera, but Lowery believed that they were authentic. The photographer had no reason to falsify them. In the interests of the survival of the species, Lowery did not say just where they were taken, but he maintained that the bird shown in the picture was "absolutely, unequivocally" an ivorybill. "I just wish I'd seen it myself; then I wouldn't give a damn how many people questioned it," he was reported as saying. Dr. Lowery made several trips with his informant to search for the birds, but they were not seen again.

The question comes up again and again: Is the ivorybill still among the living? Other ornithologists who have examined the pictures brought to Dr. Lowery agree that the bird photographed is indeed an ivory-billed woodpecker. But is it the picture of a living bird taken in the wild, they ask, or is it a mounted specimen attached to a tree?

The Search Goes On

Other undocumented sightings have been reported since that time, but the ivorybill is still as much of a will o' the wisp as ever, with no actual proof of its continued existence. One thing, however, is sure. The search will go on, for believers are spurred by the remote possibility of seeing the great woodpecker alive in its native habitat. Dr. John P. O'Neill, Director of the Museum of Natural Science at Louisiana State University since Dr. Lowery's death early in 1978, notes that he received reports of one sighting in Louisiana in 1977, and another in the spring of 1978. "I feel confident that a bird or two still exists somewhere," he says, "but the species is essentially gone."

Most other ornithologists agree. Tanner concedes that an isolated pair or an individual bird may still live in one area or another. But there is very little hope, he adds, of the species surviving for long. The remaining individuals are too scattered, and the suitable habitat too limited. Ray Erickson believes that the ivorybill should be removed from the endangered species list and be classed as extinct. If there are any verified sightings in the future, he adds, it will be easy enough to relist it among the living.

If the ivorybill does survive in one area or another, it can endure only if sufficient suitable habitat is preserved for it. Individual mature hardwood trees should be left when timber is cut, the Fish and Wildlife Service states, and pockets of cypress and other trees in wet areas should be left untouched. Softwoods, however, should be cut on a rotation basis in certain areas in order to provide a constant source of slashings for food. If a group of ivorybills should be located in any area, the Service further advises, they would be helped if a certain number of big, mature trees were girdled each year, so that there would be a constant supply of suitable dead wood in which the birds could hunt for their favorite food.

The Cuban ivorybill, a subspecies, may still survive in small numbers in Cuba, but few ornithologists believe so. The last reliable report—by John Dennis—suggested an estimated six pairs living in the mountains of Oriente Province in 1956.

Another closely related species, the imperial woodpecker, once ranged over high pine forests in the mountains of Mexico. Today its status is just as desperate and uncertain as that of its northern cousin. Its range has constantly diminished before civilization, and while in recent years there have been many rumors of the bird, there has been no positive proof of its survival.

123

7

OTHER
THREATENED
BIRDS
AND
OTHER
PROGRAMS

Many new techniques for helping endangered birds in the wild have been described in the previous chapters. Eggs or young birds may be taken from one nest and placed in another hundreds or thousands of miles away to be cared for by foster parents of the same or a different species. Whole sets of eggs may be removed and hatched in an incubator; the wild female is then often stimulated to lay another set of eggs and raise a second brood or a third. Radio transmitters may be attached to fledgling birds in order to trace their movements when they leave the nest. The examples could go on and on.

There have also been advances in the methods of breeding and raising rare birds in captivity: the use of floodlights to lengthen hours of daylight and stimulate courtship activ-

124

ities; new techniques for determining the sex of captive birds; new methods of artificial insemination. Specialized artificial diets for captive birds have been perfected for many species from hummingbirds to flamingos, from whooping crane chicks to newly hatched parrots. Vitamin and mineral supplements and the antibiotics needed for healthy growth have been determined as well.

Various ways of altering the environment to help a threatened species have also been developed. Sometimes it is enough merely to clean up—to stop the use of insecticides or the dumping of other harmful substances. Sometimes predators or parasites such as the cowbird may be removed from places where they have a harmful effect on an endangered species. Sometimes a program of supplementary feeding is helpful. The burning of jack pines to provide the specialized habitat needed by Kirtland's warbler is a classic example of man's manipulation of the environment to help a threatened species.

Many birds benefit from artificial nest boxes or nesting platforms set up especially for them. Ospreys, eagles, and other birds of prey will adopt platforms or artificial ledges set up in areas where their natural nest sites have been destroyed. Bluebirds benefit from nest boxes with an entrance hole one and a half inches in diameter, big enough for the bluebird to enter, but too small for the starling, an alien that frequently takes over natural cavities bluebirds use.

In Bermuda, the hard-pressed cahow, a storm petrel, is aided in its long-continued struggle for survival by the construction of artificial nesting burrows with doorways and baffles designed to allow the cahow to enter but not the somewhat-larger long-tailed tropic bird. This latter species often takes over the cahow's natural nest burrow and kills the cahow young.

The New Science of Clinical Ornithology

Most of these different techniques for helping endangered birds are adaptations of knowledge accumulated over the centuries by bird watchers, wildlife biologists, gamekeepers, falconers, aviculturists, and cage-bird enthusiasts. Many of the methods result from observations of the special behavior patterns of particular species in the wild; others have been perfected by curators and bird keepers in zoos and private preserves. Some are simple extensions of wildlife management techniques first taught a half century ago by Aldo Leopold at the University of Wisconsin.

Many sciences contribute to shaping programs for the preservation of threatened species: veterinary science, medicine, nutrition, ecology, animal behavior, and classical ornithology. Bird watchers and others who simply like birds and want to help them also have influence. Skill in politics and human relations, as well as plenty of dedication, is useful in setting up the programs and getting the money to run them. Different groups and individuals—both governmental and private—have a stake in the work; often they do not agree among themselves as to what should be done. However, they are all involved in a new science, which David Zimmerman calls "clinical ornithology."

The United States Fish and Wildlife Service is in the thick of the battle, with its wildlife biologists, its refuges, its recovery teams, its research programs, its facilities and personnel. State fish and game departments are rapidly becoming more active in helping endangered and nongame species, too. Such private organizations as the National Audubon Society and the National Wildlife Federation have been supporting and instituting research and active programs for years to help rare and endangered species. A number of these species have been successfully bred and raised in zoos and by such private groups as the International Crane Foundation at Baraboo, Wisconsin, and the Wildfowl Trust at Slimbridge, England.

Short accounts of some of the other programs undertaken in behalf of threatened species of American birds follow.

The Decline and Recovery of the Osprey

In the late 1950s and early 1960s, Roger Tory Peterson noted an alarming decline of the ospreys that had nested for generations along the estuaries of the Connecticut River and on the shores of Long Island Sound near his home in Old Lyme, Connecticut. Once there had been as many as 150 active nests on Great Island, at the mouth of the river. By 1961, however, they had been reduced to only thirty-one. Ten years later there were just three.

Other ornithologists noted a similar decline on the New Jersey coast, where there were only about fifty active nests in 1974 compared to nearly ten times that many before 1950. The birds were not breeding successfully in either place; fewer birds were nesting, and most of the eggs laid by those who were were not hatching. Why? The cause was the same as with so many other species—eggshell thinning and reproductive failure due to ingestion of DDT.

In 1968, a doctoral student at Cornell, Paul Spitzer, started an osprey egg-transfer experiment, exchanging eggs and nestling ospreys from a relatively noncontaminated osprey population in Chesapeake Bay with the eggs of ospreys in Long Island Sound. The Long Island Sound eggs had no better results in Chesapeake Bay nests than they had showed at home. The transferred Chesapeake Bay eggs, however, hatched just as successfully in the Long Island

Sound nests as they would have in their home nests. The Chesapeake ospreys had evidently not taken in the lethal amounts of DDT that their northern relatives had.

A similar program was undertaken along the New Jersey coast, and today there has been a comeback in both areas. A prohibition on the use of DDT, producing a steady decline in its level over the years, and the setting up of man-made nesting platforms for the birds helped, too.

Over 100 young ospreys have been raised in the Long Island Sound area in recent years. About forty young birds were fledged on the Jersey coast from 1974 through 1977. Three pairs of these birds have returned to nest and successfully raise young of their own. Active New Jersey nests have now risen to seventy or more.

The Hawaiian Goose, or Nene

Hawaii's state bird, the nene, once roamed by the thousands over the lava fields and mountain slopes of our fiftieth state. Some estimate that there were at least 25,000 of them when Captain James Cook visited Hawaii in 1778. The species had long since given up the migratory and aquatic habits of its distant ancestors, and the almost-flightless bird declined radically when civilization came to the islands. Goats and sheep and other livestock competed with the nene for food and destroyed its habitat. Cats, dogs, mongooses, and other introduced predators killed the birds for food. So did the native Polynesians and the whaling crews, visitors, and settlers that came after them. By 1949, the population of wild nenes was down to perhaps two or three dozen birds.

Herbert C. Shipman, a Hawaiian rancher, had been raising nenes in semidomestication for some years, however.

128

He provided the state with several pairs, and he also donated several breeding individuals to the Wildfowl Trust at Slimbridge, England, in 1951 and 1952. Run by Peter Scott, a world-renowned ornithologist and waterfowl expert, the Trust specialized in breeding and raising rare waterfowl. At Slimbridge, the three original birds have since multiplied to several hundred, and others have been raised by aviculturalists on private preserves.

In Hawaii, the birds were propagated at a breeding farm at Pohakuloa, on the slopes of Mauna Loa. Captured wild birds were introduced to reduce the dangers of inbreeding and to increase fertility. By 1974, some 1300 goslings had been raised at this installation alone.

Today, through arrangements with private landowners in Hawaii, three nene sanctuaries totaling about 45,000 acres have been established. In addition, the state owns another

nene

sanctuary of about 38,000 acres. Among them, these four areas include much of the old breeding habitat of the species. Since 1960, more than 1200 geese have been released in these sanctuaries, using a gentle-release technique. This method consists of placing the young captive-reared birds in open-topped enclosures about an acre in area. Stout fences keep out predators as the birds are gradually conditioned to the surrounding wild habitat. When they are ready, the nenes leave their halfway homes voluntarily and face the world on their own. Today the wild population is estimated at 750 birds or more, and many of them are breeding.

Breeding Peregrine Falcons and Releasing Them

The ongoing program to bring back the peregrine falcon in the United States and Canada is one of the most publicized and ambitious of all the breeding-and-release programs. A swift and beautiful bird of prey, the peregrine was another victim of chlorinated-hydrocarbon pesticides. During the 1950s and early 1960s it disappeared so quickly over much of its natural range that it was gone almost before anyone realized what had happened.

One of the first steps in a restoration program was taken in 1971 when Tom Cade of Cornell University's Laboratory of Ornithology raised a red-tailed hawk, which had been hatched from an egg fertilized by artificial insemination. The next year he tried the same technique on captive peregrines and succeeded. At the same time, another Cornell-trained ornithologist, Heinz Meng, bred captive peregrine falcons by natural means at New Paltz State Teachers College, New York, and raised three chicks.

Within the next several years a full-fledged program was launched. In 1973, three pairs of peregrines at Cornell produced twenty young by natural breeding. In 1974, Meng put two fledglings in an eyrie at New Paltz and continued feeding them as they were introduced to the wild by a modification of the falconer's hacking technique. Meanwhile, Cade was testing another method of reintroduction to the wild: transferring captive-bred peregrines from Cornell to the nests of wild Rocky Mountain peregrines. These foster parents successfully raised the young birds. In following years, the Cornell effort also resulted in the release by hacking of many falcons in both the East and the Rocky Mountain region.

By the spring of 1978, a total of 331 peregrines had been hatched and raised at Cornell; by the following summer, more than 130 birds had been released into the wild by hacking. Some idea of the immense amount of time and effort needed to restore the species to the East by this method, however, is demonstrated by the projections given by Cade and Stanley Temple, another falcon expert: "It will take yearly releases of 250 falcons over a fifteen-year period," they say, "to establish a wild population of 146 successfully breeding pairs in a total population of 1180 falcons."

The Canadian Wildlife Service carries on its own captive breeding program for falcons at Wainright, Alberta. Here peregrines, gyrfalcons, and prairie falcons have all been raised in captivity. Once the captive birds were breeding, removal of the first set of eggs, and sometimes the second as well, was practiced in order to stimulate the females to lay more eggs. In one experiment, eggs were placed in the nests of wild prairie falcons and Arctic peregrines, which successfully reared them.

Another technique was to remove the first clutch of eggs from the nests of wild Arctic falcons and brood them in incubators. Meanwhile, the wild females would lay another clutch. Then the first brood of incubator-hatched nestlings was placed in a nest close to the one that held the parent-incubated nestlings. The parent birds then looked after and raised both broods.

Another successful experiment involved the placing of downy peregrine young in the nests of other species of birds of prey and letting those foster parents raise them.

The Aleutian Canada Goose

One captive breeding program that has reaped large dividends is that for the Aleutian Canada goose. A small race of the Canada goose, the Aleutian subspecies traditionally bred only on the Aleutian Islands and almost disappeared entirely. The bird's downfall began more than a century ago, when first the Russians and then the Americans introduced Arctic foxes to the remote rocky islands. Besides eating goose eggs and goslings, the foxes took a high toll of the adult birds when they were in their late-summer molt and almost flightless.

Only Buldir Island had dangerous beaches for landings, and no Arctic foxes were introduced there. This tiny island, four miles long by two miles wide, remained the last stronghold of the Aleutian Canada goose. About 300 of them were counted there in 1962—probably the entire population.

In 1963, wildlife biologists captured eighteen goslings and transported them to the Monte Verde National Wildlife Refuge in Colorado. Eight of these birds were transferred to Patuxent in 1966, and a captive-breeding program was started there. Additional Buldir goslings were captured and brought to Patuxent in 1972 and 1975. Meanwhile, personnel of the Aleutian Islands National Wildlife Refuge were pursuing a program of removing foxes from Amchitka and other islands so that the Aleutian Canada goose might be introduced safely on them.

By 1971, the Patuxent flock numbered over one hundred geese, most of them bred in captivity. Seventy-five full-winged birds from one to three years old were taken to Amchitka Island and released, but all of them quickly disappeared. Another group of forty-one geese was shipped to Agattu in 1974. After a period of conditioning to the far northern land and climate, they were also released. A number of these birds survived in the wild. Five pairs were observed nesting, and several were later spotted on wintering grounds in California. A third release of about twenty captive-bred birds was made on Amchitka in 1976, but the results were uncertain. Eagles were seen preying on the birds and harassing them.

In 1976, a breeding facility was constructed at the Amchitka Fish and Wildlife headquarters and stocked with birds reared at Patuxent. An additional thirty-two goslings were reared from eggs gathered from wild nests on Buldir Island. This captive flock at Amchitka raised fifty-six young birds in 1977. A year later, more than one hundred captive-bred birds from Patuxent and Amchitka were released on Agattu after a period of conditioning.

Some seventy goslings were reared at Patuxent in 1978, and nearly one hundred on Amchitka. Some are presently being raised at the Northern Prairie Wildlife Research Center in Jamestown, North Dakota, as well. Today the total wild population of the Aleutian Canada goose is estimated to be about 1600 birds.

The Masked Bobwhite Quail

A distinctive subspecies, the masked bobwhite quail originally ranged through southern Arizona and parts of the

Mexican states of Sonora and Chihuahua. The male bird is easily distinguished by his black head and throat and an almost-solid brick-red breast. By 1900, the species had vanished in Arizona and seemed to have disappeared from most of its Mexican range as well—evidently a victim of overhunting, overgrazing, and the effects of drought on its habitat.

In 1964, a small population was rediscovered in Sonora. The Sonora Desert Museum in Arizona and several aviculturists began trying to raise the birds in captivity, but with little success. In 1966, two Arizona ornithologists, Jim and Seymour Levy, donated four pairs of their masked bobwhites to the Fish and Wildlife Service, which shipped them to Patuxent. Several years later, service biologist R. E. Tomlinson began a study of masked bobwhites in Mexico. During the course of his work, he captured a number of them and sent an additional fifty-seven to Patuxent. These birds readily adapted to captivity and soon began to breed, with no particular problems encountered.

The introduction of the captive-bred birds to the wild was another matter, however. Some 2000 Patuxent-reared bobwhites were released in Arizona between 1970 and 1974, but all of them soon disappeared. The chosen release site had been natural habitat for the quail at one time, but was now evidently unsuitable for them. The original perennial grass cover had long since been destroyed, and the area had become overgrown with mesquite and annual grasses.

In 1975, another 347 birds were put out on 1840 acres of leased ranchland by Tomlinson's successor, David H. Ellis, but again with little apparent success. The captive-bred birds were not prepared to cope with the hazards of

134

deteriorating Arizona rangeland, especially under drought conditions.

In an effort to remedy the situation, releases since 1976 have been carried out in an area where habitat improvement is being actively pursued. The method of release has been changed as well, with the introduction of covey boxes, or call-back pens. Coveys of young captive-bred quail were held in predator-proof pens at the release site in Arizona,

masked bobwhite quail

but were allowed to roam free during the day. A few confined adult quail were used to lure the coveys back into the pens for the night. Meanwhile, the young birds were conditioned to dangers in the wild by controlled harassment by people, dogs, and even hawks. After twenty-four days of such conditioning, they were released.

This covey-box training was a great improvement over previous methods, but an even more successful program followed, which incorporated the adoption of young birds by foster parents. As soon as the two-week-old chicks were received from Patuxent, they were divided into coveys of about fifteen young. Each covey was placed in an adoption chamber with an adult male Texas bobwhite that had been sterilized to avoid any hybridization. This foster parent took over the duties of brooding and looking after the young, just as an adult quail does in the wild. After one or two days in the adoption chamber to make sure that the adoption had taken, the broods were placed in following pens in dense vegetation. There they were gradually conditioned to their natural habitat. After five to ten days in the following pen, the coveys were released in the custody of their foster father. This method has resulted in successful reintroduction of many masked bobwhite to the wild.

The one remaining obstacle to the recovery of the masked bobwhite in Arizona is the lack of suitable natural habitat—the same situation that brought the species to the brink of extinction in the first place. What is sorely needed is a masked bobwhite refuge or management area where the original habitat can be restored and managed. Arrangements are being made to lease such areas, with the hope that such action will remove the last barrier to the restoration of self-sufficient populations of this unique desert species.

136

Special Requirements of the Everglade Kite

A dark-gray hawk with blood-red eyes, orange feet, and a white-banded tail, the Everglade kite is found only in the Everglades and Lake Okeechobee region of southern Florida. It builds its flimsy nest in the tall reeds and low shrubs of the watery prairies below the lake and feeds almost entirely on the big freshwater apple snail, which it skillfully extracts from its shell with its narrow, sickle-shaped bill. With such specialized requirements, the Everglade kite has almost vanished in recent years because of the drainage of marshes for agriculture and development, and the frequent manipulation of water levels in its habitat. In the mid-1960s, the Fish and Wildlife Service estimated that no more than fifteen Everglade kites remained.

The kite's nesting success has been improved in recent years, however, through the use of artificial nests. In 1973, Roderick Chandler, an Audubon warden for the Society's Lake Okeechobee Sanctuaries, observed that kite nests were so flimsy that they sometimes fell apart during high winds or rainstorms. Sometimes the nest simply caved in under the weight of the adult bird, dumping the eggs or young into the water. To prevent such casualties, Chandler began to use a woven metal basket mounted on a pipe embedded firmly in the swampy terrain. The idea of such a nest support was developed by Ivan Sutton of Pleasanton, Kansas, who brought the first models to Paul W. Sykes, Jr., a wildlife biologist with the endangered-species program. Sykes suggested their use for Everglade kites to Rod Chandler, who has used them since 1973 and improved their design.

At the beginning of the nesting season, Chandler locates a kite nest. Then he sets up a basket a few feet away and moves the nest into it. The kites readily accept the arrange-

ment, and their production has improved. In 1978, about eighty birds were counted, and from this population, eight or nine young were raised. Chandler also provides supplementary food for the kites in times of drought or low water levels, bringing in snails from distant areas and setting them out for the kites to eat.

Twelve South American snail-eating kites were brought to Patuxent in 1965–1966 so that scientists might learn how to raise Everglade kites in captivity by experimenting with these fairly common and close relatives. The project proved to be unexpectedly difficult, however, due to unsolved problems of nutrition and disease. Forty-five chicks were hatched during the next few years, but only one survived longer than six days. In 1974, with the addition of calcium carbonate to a carefully controlled diet, a young bird was finally reared successfully.

This program was phased out soon after. If it ever becomes necessary to rely on captive breeding to save the Everglade kite, however, much of the basic research has already been done. In the meantime, the outlook for safeguarding and increasing the wild population is better than it has been for a long time.

The Puerto Rican Parrot

One of many species of Amazon parrots, the Puerto Rican parrot once ranged over much of Puerto Rico, as well as Culebra and Vieques, two smaller islands lying off its east coast. No specimens were ever collected from Vieques, but three specimens of the Culebran bird, which has been described as a distinct subspecies, are preserved in museums. The parrot disappeared from both of the smaller islands by

Everglade kite

139

1800 or before, leaving only the main race on Puerto Rico. Over the years, its numbers have steadily dwindled.

Once widespread in forested areas, the surviving birds are now found only in the Luquillo National Forest near the east coast. Today this lush rain forest consists of some 28,000 acres, of which only about 5000 acres are still virgin.

About two hundred parrots were still living in Luquillo in 1950. By 1968, the number had dwindled to perhaps twenty-five; three years later the total population was thought to be no more than fifteen or twenty. These few survivors were hard pressed by the predation of red-tailed hawks, the scarcity of suitable nesting cavities, and the destruction of eggs and young by the pearly-eyed thrasher, a common and aggressive rain-forest neighbor.

A small number of the parrots have been kept in captivity during the past few years with the hope that they may eventually breed. Most were taken as young birds, and by 1976 were approaching breeding age. Today the captives number about fifteen, all of them housed at the Fish and Wildlife Service's Puerto Rican field station at Luquillo. One captive pair laid three fertile eggs in 1978, but none of the young survived. The outlook for future breeding success in captivity, however, seems promising.

Noel Snyder, Jim Wiley, and Cameron Kepler—all biologists with the Fish and Wildlife Service—and their associates that work for the Puerto Rican Forest Service and the Commonwealth Department of Natural Resources have improved the chances for the nesting success of the wild birds in several different ways. One is by deepening natural nesting cavities and by adding visorlike rain shelters or caps to prevent flooding. Another is by providing artificial nest sites in territories of parrots that have lacked good natural nest cavities.

One common problem in the past has been the pre-empting of parrot nests by the pearly-eyed thrasher. This competition has been reduced by providing the thrashers with artificial nest sites and by adapting other sites so that only the parrots will use them. The thrashers are quite reluctant to descend into deep holes with bottoms that are not visible. Such holes, however, suit the parrots very well.

Another technique that helps the parrots breed success-fully has been the removal of eggs from the nests when they are laid and the substitution of plaster eggs. The removed eggs are hatched under an incubator, and the young cared for until they are two weeks old. Having successfully passed through the most critical stage, they are then returned to their parents for rearing.

"The present status of the parrot is actually quite en-couraging," Snyder noted in the fall of 1978. "The field program, which is currently under the direction of Jim Wiley, had great success this year, and the population in the wild has shown an encouraging spurt upward. Nine young parrots fledged in the wild this spring, bringing the wild population up to a minimum of twenty-six and a maximum of twenty-eight. . . . Our biggest concern now is that Puerto Rico be spared any hurricanes for a few years. The difficulties the birds have been having with nest sites and with predation by thrashers now appear to be over."

Attwater's Prairie Chicken

A great many endangered species—probably the majority of them—are in that predicament because much of the hab-itat that they need for survival has been drastically altered or destroyed by man. Attwater's prairie chicken, a sub-species of the greater prairie chicken (which is also en-

141

dangered) is an example. This bird once lived in some 300 miles of coastal Texas prairie, ranging from the Louisiana border to the Rio Grande and extending inland for about 100 miles. Early in the century, when it was plentiful, Attwater's prairie chicken was overhunted. Overgrazing, controlled burning to clear the land of brush, and the draining of much of the land for agriculture steadily reduced suitable habitat to less than a tenth of what it was originally. Where there had once been six million acres of good territory for the Attwater's prairie chicken, there were just one-half million acres in 1937, with fewer than 9000 birds living there. By 1967, the habitat had been reduced to about 234,000 acres and the birds numbered little more than 1000.

Attwater's prairie chicken

That September a hurricane flooded much of the region, and the population of the Attwater's prairie chicken dropped even further. The next year, in a fund-raising effort sponsored by the World Wildlife Fund and the Nature Conservancy, 3450 acres of prime habitat was purchased and set aside for the bird as the Eagle Lake Sanctuary. This land was later purchased by the Fish and Wildlife Service, which now administers it as the Attwater Prairie Chicken National Wildlife Refuge. Over the years, the refuge area has been expanded to about 8000 acres. The population of Attwater's prairie chickens on the refuge has shown a gradual increase during the past several years, and now totals about 150 birds. Aransas is another federal refuge that supports significant numbers of this endangered form. The total present population is about 1500 birds, located in ten different counties in Texas.

"Throughout Texas," notes Wayne Shifflet, manager of the Attwater Prairie Chicken National Wildlife Refuge, "the population has been showing a gradual decline in numbers as urbanization replaces grasslands, and changes in land-use patterns contribute to the additional loss of grasslands. . . . As more pressure is exerted on private ranches to break their lands into smaller parcels, the Attwater Prairie Chicken Refuge may very well be the last place where the species may be preserved."

Hawaiian Birds

Captain James Cook discovered Hawaii for the Western world in 1778, but the Polynesians had colonized the islands hundreds of years before. Ruling over a Pacific paradise, their chiefs often wore colorful robes made of the red-and-yellow feathers of Hawaiian honeycreepers, a unique family of birds found nowhere else in the world.

143

At the time of Captain Cook's arrival, the Hawaiian Islands boasted thirty-four full species of birds and thirty-five subspecies that had evolved in the islands. Today twenty-three of those native Hawaiian birds are probably extinct, and at least twenty-seven of the rest are endangered. They make up more than half of the entire United States list of endangered birds.

The Hawaiian record for endangered species is the world's worst for island areas, with the possible exception of Madagascar. All the wildlife species on an island are forced to live together in a strictly limited habitat. They compete with one another for food and living space, and any change in the situation, such as the introduction of alien species, is likely to upset the delicate environmental balance. When that natural balance is disturbed, the native forms are the ones that usually suffer the most.

That situation is what developed in Hawaii. Westerners came, bringing goats and sheep and pigs, cats and dogs and mongooses, and many other exotic animals. Scores of birds were introduced from other lands and continents—twenty different kinds since 1965 alone. Native forests were cut for their timber or cleared for the growing of pineapple, rice, and other agricultural crops. Over 4000 kinds of alien plants were brought in from other parts of the world. No wonder that native animals and plants were lost in the shuffle, pushed under in the competition with exotics and the bulldozing of the natural environment.

The Hawaiian Islands National Wildlife Refuge, established in 1909, gave protection to some 300,000 acres of the Leewards and other islands of the chain that stretched for 1200 miles across the Pacific, north and west of the main islands. Today this refuge protects many seabird colonies as well as a number of island races of birds.

Only remnants of unspoiled habitat remain on the five main islands. Fish and Wildlife biologists are working in these areas to save as many of the endangered species and as much of the unspoiled habitat as they can. The work is sometimes discouraging, but it has its exciting moments, too. On one trip to Maui in 1967, service biologist Winston Banko rediscovered the Maui nukupuu, a bird that had been considered extinct since 1896. On that same trip he also spotted a specimen of the Maui parrotbill, a species that had been seen only once before in this century. Since

Hawaiian honeycreeper

those exciting discoveries, the Nature Conservancy has been working to acquire and preserve this area, which borders Haleakala National Park, and which the Polynesians call the Valley of the Sacred Pools. Another remarkable ornithological event was the discovery, in 1973, of an entirely new species of honeycreeper, the po-o-ali, in the Hana rain forest on the slopes of Haleakala volcano. This bird was first sighted by a group of students working on an ecological study of the area.

The program to help the surviving native wildlife of the Hawaiian Islands goes on. Some refuges have been set aside, but many others are needed on all of the main islands. In the forests, transit trails are often made and marked at intervals so the birds seen or heard at each spot can be counted. On the big island of Hawaii, one endangered honeycreeper, the palila, is being helped by the eradication of feral sheep and goats that threaten to destroy the last of the limited habitat still available to the species on the slopes of Mauna Kea volcano.

The preservation of suitable habitat is the main requirement for the endangered wildlife in Hawaii today—that and a serious effort to control and limit the many exotic plants and animals that have upset the balance.

The Death of a Species Is Forever

The rush to develop land and destroy habitat continues not only in Hawaii, but in many other parts of the world as well: the rain forests of Brazil, the jungles of the Philippine Islands and New Guinea, the African plains and forests. Alaska, the last largely unspoiled frontier left in the United States, is hard pressed today by those who are determined to develop and reap its natural resources for profit.

146

Speaking of this threat in the summer of 1978, Secretary of the Interior Cecil Andrus stated: "The Endangered Species Act . . . is only one more effort to keep open the options for future generations of people. . . . It takes a lot of conceit to assume that our generation has the right to foreclose major choices which future Americans will want to make for themselves. Once they are ravaged, vulnerable Alaskan ecosystems may never recover. And the death of a species is forever."

The efforts to save endangered birds buy time if nothing else for all of those threatened species. For many of them it means the difference between survival and extinction. If such efforts had been taken for the passenger pigeon and the Carolina parakeet, as they easily could have been, those birds would still be with us today.

The death of a species is forever. May we only realize that while there is still time—not just for endangered wildlife, but also for ourselves and all those who follow us.

147

COMMON
AND
SCIENTIFIC
NAMES

FOREWORD

Labrador duck * *Camptorhynchus labradorium*
passenger pigeon * *Ectopistes migratorius*
heath hen * *Tympanuchus cupido cupido*
eskimo curlew *Numenius borealis*

1 THE WHOOPING CRANE
Whooping crane *Grus americana*
greater sandhill crane *Grus canadensis tabida*

2 THE BALD EAGLE
northern bald eagle *Haliaeetus leucocephalus alascanus*

---

* Extinct

148

southern bald eagle
  Haliaeetus leucocephalus leucocephalus
golden eagle   *Aquila chrysaetos*

3 THE BROWN PELICAN
eastern brown pelican   *Pelecanus occidentalis carolinensis*
West Indian brown pelican
  Pelecanus occidentalis occidentalis
western brown pelican   *Pelecanus occidentalis californicus*
western grebe   *Aechmophorus occidentalis*

4 THE CALIFORNIA CONDOR
California condor   *Gymnogyps californianus*
South American or Andean condor   *Vultur gryphus*

5 THE KIRTLAND'S WARBLER
Kirtland's warbler   *Dendroica kirtlandii*
brown-headed cowbird   *Molothrus ater*

6 THE IVORY-BILLED WOODPECKER
American ivory-billed woodpecker
  Campophilus principalis principalis
pileated woodpecker   *Drycopus pileatus*
Cuban ivory-billed woodpecker
  Campophilus principalis bairdii
imperial woodpecker   *Campophilus imperialis*

7 OTHER THREATENED BIRDS
cahow   *Pterodroma cahow*
American osprey   *Pandion haliaetus carolinensis*
Hawaiian goose or nene   *Branta sandvicensis*
American peregrine falcon   *Falco peregrinus anatum*
Arctic peregrine falcon   *Falco peregrinus tundrius*

gyrfalcon *Falco rusticolus*
prairie falcon *Falco mexicanus*
masked bobwhite *Colinus virginianus ridgwayi*
Texas bobwhite *Colinus virginianus texanus*
Florida Everglade or snail kite
  Rostrhamus sociabilis plumbeus
South American snail kite
  Rostrhamus sociabilis sociabilis
Puerto Rican parrot *Amazona vittata vittata*
Culebran Amazon parrot * *Amazona vittata gracilipes*
Attwater's greater prairie chicken
  Tympanuchus cupido attwateri
northern greater prairie chicken
  Tympanuchus cupido pinnatus
Maui nukupuu *Hemignathus lucidus affinus*
Maui parrotbill *Pseudonestor xanthophrys*
po-o-ali *Melamprosops phaeosoma*
palila *Psittirostra bailleui*

SELECTED
BIBLIOGRAPHY

Publications of the Fish and Wildlife Service (United States Department of the Interior) have been very helpful in the preparation of this work—particularly the many news releases, technical bulletins, annual reports, and review or final drafts of recovery plans prepared by the recovery teams for the whooping crane, eastern brown pelican, California condor, Kirtland's warbler, and masked bobwhite. Among the most useful general magazines that were checked for up-to-date information on the subject were *Audubon Magazine* (National Audubon Society); *Animal Kingdom* (New York Zoological Society); *National Wildlife* (National Wildlife Federation); and *Smithsonian* (The Smithsonian Institution). The titles that follow should be of interest to any reader who wishes to pursue a particular subject further.

Allen, Robert P., *The Whooping Crane*. (Research Report No. 3) New York, National Audubon Society, 1952.

———, *The Whooping Crane's Northern Breeding Grounds*. (A Supplement to Research Report No. 3) New York, National Audubon Society, 1956.

Audubon, John James, *Ornithological Biography, or an Account of the Habits of the Birds of the United States of America*. Vol. I. Philadelphia, E. L. Carey and A. Hart, 1832. Vol. II. Boston, Hilliard, Gray, and Company, 1835. (A modern edition of this work, selected and edited by Alice Ford, was published in 1957 by the Macmillan Company, New York).

Broley, Myrtle Jean, *Eagle Man*. New York, Pellegrini and Cudahy, 1952.

Bent, Arthur Cleveland, *Life Histories of North American Birds*. (20 Vols.) Bulletin, U.S. National Museum, 1919–1958.

No. 121. Petrels and Pelicans and their Allies, 1922.
No. 135. North American Marsh Birds, 1926.
No. 167. Birds of Prey, Part 1, 1937.
No. 170. Birds of Prey, Part 2, 1938.
No. 174. Woodpeckers, 1939.
No. 203. North American Wood Warblers, 1953.

(All of these have been published in paperback by Dover Publications, Inc., New York)

Conway, William G., "A Different Kind of Captivity." *Animal Kingdom*, Vol. 81, No. 2 (April/May 1978), pp. 4-9.

Dennis, John V., "The Ivorybill Flies Still." *Audubon*, Vol. 69, No. 6 (November, 1967), pp. 38-44.

Defenders of Wildlife, *Defenders*, Vol. 50, No. 6 (December, 1975), pp. 476-481, 491-496, 506-511, 525-528. (A special issue on Hawaiian wildlife).

152

Fisher, James, Simon, Noel, and Vincent, Jack, *Wildlife in Danger*. New York, The Viking Press, 1969.

Ford, Alice, ed., *The Bird Biographies of John James Audubon*. New York, The Macmillan Company, 1957.

Graham, Frank, Jr., "Endangered Birds: Tinkering for Time." *Audubon*, Vol. 79, No. 6 (November, 1977), pp. 137-141.

————, *Since Silent Spring*. Boston, Houghton Mifflin Company, 1970. (Also a Fawcett Crest paperback).

Greenway, James C., *Extinct and Vanishing Birds of the World*. New York, American Committee for International Wildlife Protection, 1958.

Harrison, George H., "Crane Saviors of Baraboo." *Audubon*, Vol. 80, No. 2 (March, 1978), pp. 25-28.

King, Kirke A., Flickinger, Edward L., and Hildebrand, Henry H., "The Decline of Brown Pelicans on the Louisiana and Texas Gulf Coast." *The Southwest Naturalist*, Vol. 21, No. 4 (February 10, 1977), pp. 417-431.

Koford, Carl B., *The California Condor*. (Research Report No. 4) New York, National Audubon Society, 1953.

Laycock, George, *Autumn of the Eagle*. New York, Charles Scribner's Sons, 1973.

Mayfield, Harold, *The Kirtland's Warbler*. Michigan, Cranbrook Institute of Science, 1960.

Mackenzie, John P.S., *Birds in Peril*. Boston, Houghton Mifflin Company, 1977.

McCoy, J. J., *The Hunt for the Whooping Cranes*. New York, Lothrop, Lee & Shepard Co., Inc., 1966.

McMillan, Ian, *Man and the California Condor*. New York, E. P. Dutton & Co. Inc., 1968.

McNulty, Faith, "Last Days of the Condor?" *Audubon*, Vol. 80, No. 2 (March, 1978), p. 53-87, Part 1; and Vol. 80, No. 3 May, 1978), pp. 78–100, Part 2.

———, "The Silent Shore." *Audubon*, Vol. 73, No. 6 (November, 1971), pp. 5-11.

———, *The Whooping Crane; The Bird that Defies Extinction*. New York, E. P. Dutton & Co. Inc., 1966.

Nevin, David, "The Irresistible Elusive Allure of the Ivory-bill." *Smithsonian*, Vol. 4, No. 11 (February, 1974), pp. 72-81.

Ossa, Helen, *They Saved Our Birds; The Battle Won and the War to Win*. New York, Hippocrene Books, 1973.

Riciutti, Edward R. "Deathwatch at Patuxent." *Audubon*, Vol. 81, No. 1 (January, 1979), pp. 82-92.

Sayre, Roxanna, "Panel: Condor Needs Research, Large-scale Captive Breeding." *Audubon*, Vol. 80, No. 5 (September, 1978), pp. 136-143.

Schreiber, Ralph W., "Bad Days for the Brown Pelican." *National Geographic*, Vol. 147, No. 1 (January, 1975), pp. 111-123.

Schueler, Donald, "Incident at Eagle Ranch." *Audubon*, Vol. 80, No. 3 (May, 1978), pp. 41-72.

Tanner, James T., *The Ivory-billed Woodpecker*. (Research Report No. 1) New York, National Audubon Society, 1942.

Temple, Stanley A., ed. *Endangered Birds: Management Techniques for Preserving Threatened Species*. Madison, Wisconsin, University of Wisconsin Press, 1977.

Wilson, Alexander, *American Ornithology; or the Natural History of the Birds of the United States*. 3 Vols. London, Whittaker, Treacher, and Arnot, 1832.

Zimmerman, David R., "A Technique Called Cross-fostering May Help Save the Whooping Crane." *Smithsonian*, Vol. 9, No. 6 (September, 1978), pp. 52-63.

———, *To Save a Bird in Peril*. New York, Coward, McCann & Geoghegan, Inc., 1975.

INDEX

Species are indexed by their common names. Scientific names are listed on pages 148-50. An asterisk indicates an illustration.

155